IN SEARCH OF POLAND

IN SEARCH OF POLAND

The Superpowers' Response to Solidarity, 1980-1989

Arthur R. Rachwald

Hoover Institution Press

Stanford University
Stanford, California

This study was made possible thanks to a grant under the Discretionary Grant Program of the Department of State, pursuant to the Soviet-Eastern European Research and Training Act of 1983, Public Law 98–164, Title VIII, 97 Stat. 1047–50.

Hoover Press Publication 396

First printing, 1990
96 95 94 93 92 91 90   9 8 7 6 5 4 3 2 1
Simultaneous first paperback printing, 1990
96 95 94 93 92 91 90   9 8 7 6 5 4 3 2 1

Manufactured in the United States of America
Printed on acid-free paper

Library of Congress Cataloging-in-Publication Data
Rachwald, Arthur R.
   In search of Poland : the superpowers' response to Solidarity,
1980–1989 / Arthur R. Rachwald.
        p.   cm.
   Includes bibliographical references.
   ISBN 0–8179–8961–7 (alk. paper)
   ISBN 0–8179–8962–5 (pbk. : alk. paper)
   1. Poland—Foreign relations—1945–1989. 2. Soviet Union—Foreign relations—Poland. 3. Poland—Foreign relations—Soviet Union.
4. United States—Foreign relations—Poland. 5. Poland—Foreign relations—United States. 6. NSZZ "Solidarność" (Labor organization) 7. Poland—Politics and government—1980–1989.
I. Title.
DK4442.R33 1990   90–4551
327'.09438—dc20   CIP

Contents

Foreword

The second half of the twentieth century has been characterized not only by rapidly developing technology, but also by massive displacements of governmental systems as many nations have successfully freed themselves from alien political, economic, and cultural values. This global process of national self-determination, begun after World War II, produced rapid decolonialization of overseas empires. By the end of the 1980s the governments of Western Europe had shed their colonies and begun to focus their attention on social problems and national security.

During the first decades following the end of the Second World War, the USSR appeared immune to the national aspirations of peoples subjugated by communism. Thus decolonialization in the West went hand in hand with an expanding Soviet empire. In the 1950s and 1960s, Moscow succeeded in suppressing several national uprisings in Central Europe; during the 1970s it expressed global aspirations and proclaimed the unilateral right to issue ideological, political, and military proclamations anywhere in the world. The Soviet grip over other nations remained secure because subjugated peoples knew that military force (the so-called Brezhnev Doctrine of limited sovereignty) would prevent any deviations from Marxism-Leninism.

The last decade of Poland's struggle against USSR domination began with the August 1980 agreement between the communist government in Warsaw and the first independent and self-governing trade union in the

Soviet bloc, namely, Solidarity. Moscow's response to this historic challenge to its authority included a variety of measures aimed at suppressing and discrediting this spontaneous social and nationwide movement. The Kremlin used ideological and political harassment, economic sanctions, direct threats of armed intervention, and, eventually, a military solution via proxies to pressure the union and the communist authorities in Warsaw. Professor Rachwald's study examines the sequence, intensity, and temporary effectiveness of the USSR's resistance to the first successful anticolonial movement within the "socialist commonwealth of nations."

The author's analysis of lengthy encounters between martial law authorities and Solidarity in the years following the 13 December 1981 crackdown on the union portrays Soviet failure to contain or reverse the political aspirations of the Polish people. The utility of force was neutralized by the nation's refusal to cooperate with or support economic reforms sponsored by the regime. Nine years of struggle against communism in Poland had been socially and economically devastating. At the end, however, Moscow was forced to capitulate. Semifree elections in June 1989 brought into power a Solidarity-led coalition and caused the former ruling communist party to dissolve on 27 January 1990.

United States policies toward the key political players in Warsaw were a critical factor in the Polish-Soviet struggle during the 1980s. Driven by both strategic considerations and sympathy for the prodemocracy objectives of the opposition, the United States offered a comprehensive package of incentives designed to promote Solidarity. Equally extensive disincentives were set up to discourage Moscow and Warsaw from using force or other forms of repression against the union.

Besides relations with the regime in Warsaw, for the first time since the establishment of communist rule in Poland, the United States opened direct contacts with the political opposition. Washington cultivated this relationship despite Solidarity's delegalization by the military junta. United States support for the union, combined with the significant U.S. economic sanctions, led to the final breakdown of the communist politico-economic system.

An analysis of the complexities of Soviet and U.S. policies during said crisis would not be complete without reference to the internal debate on the new domestic and international profile of Poland. The third part of Professor Rachwald's study examines Polish politics within the context of international affairs, focusing on the ways and means communist authorities used to protect the system from its ultimate collapse. Repeated failures of economic reforms and continuous attempts to refurbish the political facade become especially meaningful when viewed from the background of Warsaw's relations with Moscow and Washington. For years both the communist regime in Poland and Solidarity walked a tight-rope between the superpowers in an attempt to maximize their political prospects and minimize antagonism with the outside world as well as with their domestic constituencies. An inquiry into this protracted rivalry is skillfully presented by the author, a recognized expert on the intricacies of politics in Poland.

Professor Rachwald has achieved this insight into the nuances of Polish politics through extensive reliance on original source materials. The book is the more valuable because it critically evaluates government documents, official statements, treaties, declarations, and letters related to the subject. The quality of this wealth of original material ensures that this study will occupy a unique place in the literature of Solidarity both at home and abroad.

Richard F. Staar
Coordinator,
International Studies Program
Hoover Institution

Introduction

Until 1989, Poland was a product of the international system that resulted from the division of Europe at the conclusion of World War II. The necessities of geopolitics have repeatedly been challenged by the Polish people, who by and large have viewed the communist system imposed by Moscow as alien to the national tradition and a barrier to socioeconomic progress. The communist order in Poland has several times come under spontaneous popular pressure, forcing the authorities to implement major ideological, political, and economic adjustments to the patterns transplanted from Moscow.

This continuing friction between the aspirations of the Polish people and the exigencies of the international system has long been a major source of tension between the superpowers, and has elevated Poland's internal situation to international status. The country is under close scrutiny by Moscow and Washington, both aware that the struggle for the final socioeconomic profile of Poland is not over yet, and that its outcome will have a direct impact on the balance of power in Europe.

The appearance in Poland of a trade union that was free and independent (from the communist authorities) met with strong reactions in both the East and the West. Moscow perceived Solidarity as the most destabilizing challenge to its imperial order in Eastern Europe since Titoism in 1948. Soviet strategy in dealing with the crisis was characterized by a stubborn determination to destroy Solidarity, accompanied by considerable flexibility on the question of how and when to execute that destruction. The possibility of a Soviet military invasion of Poland was not ruled out; but the Soviet leaders were deterred by the anticipated consequences of a war with Poland. They accepted, with reservations, the idea of martial law. This internal solution was a face-saving one for Moscow, but it also denied the Soviet leaders direct control over Polish events, such as they had had after the Hungarian and Czechoslovakian uprisings.

For the United States, the Polish crisis opened new opportunities for a peaceful engagement in this traditionally pro-U.S. nation. There was an expectation that Poland would move toward a more balanced position between East and West. The Polish regime was given generous support as long as it was willing to respect the human rights of the Polish people; this support was terminated, however, once the experiment with the independent union was cut short by the internal invasion carried out by Gen. Wojciech Jaruzelski. The imposition of martial law in Poland was followed by economic sanctions applied against the Polish regime. It was calculated that the West's economic pressure eventually would induce the martial law authorities to restore civil rights and liberties.

The domestic dimension of the Polish crisis involved complex relations among three political players: the communist authorities, the Catholic church, and the opposition. Each of these organizations in Poland was linked to foreign centers of support in addition to having domestic roots and support. The political successes or failures of each group automatically determined the degree of a particular foreign influence in Poland. Martial law secured the priority of Soviet interests in Poland, but it also preserved the liberal and pluralistic character of the Polish system. In the long run it proved ineffective in its attempt to stop Poland's evolution away from the Soviet model.

The search for a socioeconomic system in Poland is likely to continue for the foreseeable future—until the country develops an acceptable and functional socioeconomic structure. The drama of Solidarity is not over yet, as the Polish nation continues to experiment with alternative political and economic solutions and tries to rediscover its political tradition and adapt it to modern circumstances.

The 1980–89 crisis in Poland may turn out to have been the last major, protracted cold war battle in Europe, involving competition by the two superpowers over the international orientation and domestic system in one of the major nations of Europe. It may not be prudent to assert that it was a zero-sum game between Moscow and Washington, and that the Russians lost the cold war; but it is certainly fair to say that the 1980–89 workers' uprising in Poland tipped the scale in the historical duel between democracy and Marxist-Leninist totalitarianism.

PART I

Solidarity and the USSR

CHAPTER ONE

Moscow and the Independent Trade Union in Poland

Poland's 1980 revolt shook the foundations of the communist system in the entire Soviet bloc. Unlike the upheavals in Hungary (1956) and Czechoslovakia (1968), which were initiated by the liberal wings of those countries' ruling communist elites, the driving force in Poland has been the working class, whose principal goal is emancipation from the communist dictatorship. The Polish workers have broken one of the key axioms of the Soviet system—the assertion that the communist party has the exclusive right to represent the working class. The appearance of an independent and noncommunist trade union—a genuine representation of the working class—was a direct challenge to the party's "leading role," and automatically a threat to Soviet supremacy in Poland.

The priority of Soviet interests in Poland is guaranteed by the political monopoly of the communist party. Its power rests on three pillars: the party's leading role in all aspects of social and economic life, enhanced by its *nomenklatura* system of appointments; the principle of democratic centralism, which serves as the main guarantor of strict internal party discipline; and the comprehensive system of censorship. The idea of an independent labor organization functioning freely is totally incompatible with the Soviet system. From the beginning, the autonomous union assumed a political character: it replaced the party as a representative of the Polish working class; it objected to the *nomenklatura*, which had hermetically closed the system to any grass-roots influence; and it shattered Soviet censorship by acquiring the right to publish union newspapers that would not be censored.

The Soviets were immediately alarmed. Moscow's biggest fear was that pluralism would undermine the myth of the communist party's historical right to speak for the working class. It threatened the legitimacy of the communist authorities, who had conquered political power but had never won free elections. The communist rulers claimed the right to provide the sole representation of not only the working class, but the entire nation. Any attempt to restrain their absolutism could trigger a chain reaction that might ultimately prove fatal to the system. The communist party was profoundly distrustful of any spontaneous initiatives that could become irreversible steps toward political pluralism. The Polish workers' insurrection against the communist party and the prospect of pluralism taking hold in the largest Soviet satellite in Eastern Europe put the Soviets on alert.

Moreover, Poland provides Russia with access to Europe. Without direct control over Poland, the Russian rulers—whether "red" or "white"—are barred from European politics and placed in an Asian cultural environment. Russian czars and Soviet first secretaries alike have pursued heavy-handed imperial policies toward Poland, which is known for its Western culture and its history of rabid, anti-Russian nationalism. Poland is also fervently Catholic, and has a homogeneous population approaching 40 million.

As a Soviet satellite, Poland became famous for its assiduous resistance to Sovietization. The October 1956 revolt of the Polish workers terminated Stalinism and introduced the "national road to socialism," a concept of socialist development that did not require a cloning of the Soviet experience. Another major revolt in Poland, the 1970 riots in Gdańsk, was brutally suppressed by the police; but the new leadership recognized the necessity of providing consumer goods as a work incentive, and was the first in the Soviet bloc to initiate a system of socialist consumerism. Unfortunately for the communists, Poland's high standard of living was made possible by the easy availability of Western credits rather than by the performance of the Polish economy. This led to political tremors in 1976, culminating with the workers' decision to organize independently of the party—a direct assault on the communist system. The formation of the Solidarity union was an ominous symptom of disorder in the imperial Soviet system. Although the struggle was between the union and the Polish communist party, the creation of Solidarity was in essence an act of defiance against Moscow.

The Polish revolt was a serious issue not only because the working class of a socialist state was revolting against communist rule, but because the revolt was taking place when serious economic problems had begun to surface throughout the entire Soviet bloc. The communist regimes were losing control of their economies and labor forces. Most of the economic difficulties of the other bloc states were similar to those of Poland; thus economic stagnation in Eastern Europe could spread to the entire region. Moreover, a very discouraging economic outlook for all socialist economies was giving a strong impetus to political instability.

Official silence was the first Soviet reaction to the emergence of Solidarity. In the weeks before the 20 August 1980 agreement between the Polish government and the union, the Soviet media ignored the Polish problem.

The first reference to the Polish crisis was made by *Pravda* in its comments on a speech delivered by Polish United Workers' Party leader Edward Gierek on the labor unrest in Poland. Carefully avoiding any reference to strikes, negotiations between Solidarity and the Polish government, or the economic crisis in Poland, *Pravda* called attention to an alleged "effort to make use of work stoppages to serve hostile political goals . . . by irresponsible, anarchistic, and anti-socialist elements."[1]

The Soviet statement on the Polish crisis revealed Moscow's perception of the events in Poland. The Soviets assumed that the communist system in Poland worked well, but that a supposed Western intervention in Poland's internal affairs was causing difficulties. While Moscow was preparing a propaganda case for the eventual invasion of Poland, the Polish authorities wasted no time in reminding the Polish people that political concessions have limits. Poland's political geography is such that the country's independence was limited and was contingent on the communist monopoly of power in Poland and on membership in the Warsaw Pact. The communist system in Poland is dictated by *raison d'état;* as the Polish leaders like to reiterate: "Only a socialist Poland can be a free and independent country with inviolable borders." This is to say that the Warsaw regime would never be willing to cede so much that the Soviets were provoked to invade. Eventually the specter of the Red Army moving into Poland to crush a spontaneous social movement was a clear and present danger that haunted Polish citizens and brought a halt to the experiment with free unions.

In fact, the Soviet response to the Polish crisis followed a standard formula, accusing the United States of imperialistic interference in the domestic affairs of Poland, accusing the Federal Republic of Germany of having revanchist intentions, and drawing a direct parallel between the events in Czechoslovakia in 1968 and developments in Poland in 1980.

It was ironical, therefore, that at the time when the Polish workers were revolting against the communist party, *Trybuna ludu,* the Central

Committee's daily, felt obligated to praise the rebels for the "maturity of the Polish working class [that] consists among other things in the fact that even in an atmosphere of conflict and the excitement connected with it this class did not lend an ear to the instigation undermining the foundations of the socialist system." In addition, it said that the "unbreakable alliance with the USSR and the organic ties linking Poland with the entire community of socialist states in all spheres of life also belong to the Polish principles. These fraternal bonds are the foundation of the political mentality of Polish society."[2]

At the same time, the Polish authorities selected two prominent political activists in Poland—Jacek Kuron and Adam Michnik—as prime examples of antisocialist activities directed by the West. While the Polish press continued to express confidence in the ability of the Polish workers and the party to settle their differences within the socialist political framework, Kuron and Michnik were accused of sponsoring the antisocialist campaign, and of attempting to exploit the conflict so as to alter the domestic political system and loosen Poland's ties to the Soviet Union and the other Soviet-bloc states.

The Committee for the Defense of Workers, a group of intellectuals organized in 1976 to assist imprisoned workers, was portrayed by the regime as an imperialist fifth column, sponsoring political activities that jeopardized Poland's security. The committee was accused of undermining socialism from inside, by penetrating the Polish working class and using its legitimate demands and its discontent in furtherance of Western interests. In the official view, therefore, the Polish revolt had two aspects: first, a genuine expression of workers' concern about Poland's economic situation; and second, open or disguised antisocialist activities aimed at detaching Poland from the Soviet bloc. In the communist jargon, some elements of the Polish situation had a counterrevolutionary character. This dual approach to Solidarity was designed to please both the Polish workers and the Soviet leaders. It gave Warsaw flexibility either to decide that a particular economic demand was legitimate, or to accuse the union of tampering with politics.

This dualism was absent from the Soviet perception of Polish events. The Soviet leaders disliked Solidarity and its August 1980 settlement with the Polish communist party. For the Soviets, the settlement represented a loss of the communist party monopoly on political power, a demonstration of the Polish leadership's weakness, and the deformation of a socialist state, which should never permit the workers to organize or grant concessions to them. To show its displeasure with the Polish concessions, *Pravda* published several editorials signed by "Alexey Petrov," a Kremlin pseudonym, expressing the Soviet leadership's views. Solidarity was linked with "subversive centers" in the West and defined as an antisocialist force that had infiltrated a number of Polish enterprises. On 1 September 1980, Petrov wrote that the "antisocialist elements" in Poland "ignore the fact that [strikes] poison the political atmosphere in the country and threaten the emergence of anarchy in public life, and they ignore the possible consequences for the state and the people."

A more direct attack on Solidarity was expressed in Petrov's 20 September article, which linked the union to the United States and various West German political organizations, all desperately trying to "turn backward the development of the People's Poland, to push it off the socialist path and to redraw the postwar map of Europe." Still, Moscow continued to support the Polish communist party, crediting it with a "program for further development of the country" and the ability to "consolidate the ties of the party with the people and the working class." Finally, on 27 September, *Pravda* reminded the Poles that their state exists only at the Soviets' pleasure, and that the Soviet system in Poland is "guaranteed by the fraternal unity with the other socialist countries."

Despite the Soviet leaders' irritation with the performance of the Polish regime, Moscow apparently still hoped for an early emasculation or takeover of Solidarity by the communist regime. Personnel changes in the Polish communist hierarchy, announced in early September 1980, were promptly approved by Moscow in hopes that the new Polish chief, Stanisław Kania, would show more determination in dealing with the workers than Edward Gierek. Kania's credentials impressed Moscow: for a decade before his elevation to the position of first secretary, he was responsible for internal security, and thus was expected to take a hard line with the opposition.

The Soviets' endorsement of Kania included approval of his advocacy of the leading role of the communist party and commitment to the "inviolable friendship" between Poland and the Soviet Union.[3] Moscow expected the new Polish leadership to regain political momentum, pacify the workers, and stabilize the economy.

These expectations were reiterated by the Soviet leadership when Stanisław Kania and Jozef Pinkowski, Poland's new premier, flew to Moscow for a short audience with the Soviet leadership. The five-hour meeting at the Kremlin resulted in full Soviet endorsement of Kania's efforts to contain Solidarity, which by then claimed seven million supporters. After the Polish leaders departed, Radio Moscow stated:

L. I. Brezhnev expressed the conviction of Soviet Communists, workers of the Soviet Union, that Communists, workers of fraternal Poland, will be able to resolve the acute economic development facing them and, re-

lying on the material and spiritual potential created during the years of
the people's power, ensure the growth of the workers' standard of living
as well as the further, all-round progress of People's Poland.[4]

The new leadership had gained more time to restore Soviet-like order
in Poland, before the Soviets would do it for them. Despite deep anxieties,
Moscow was still inclined to believe that the Polish communist regime
had enough residual strength to handle the crisis. Besides political support, the Soviets had given the regime 500,000 tons of food and consumer
goods, plus a $150 million hard currency credit.[5] This was in addition to
$690 million in credits already granted by the Soviet government and
$150 million provided by East Germany. The Soviet Union and its East
European allies began to feel the economic burden of the Polish crisis.[6]
Ultimately, Moscow had to pay for the economic concessions made by the
Polish government to its working class.

The cadre changes and the economic assistance from the West—including $670 million provided by the United States and DM 1.2 billion
given by West Germany—were accepted by Moscow as a necessary way
out of a difficult and embarrassing situation. The Soviets expected the Polish problem to be resolved by the new Polish authorities without delay
and without the use of force. Moscow was prepared to tolerate some political concessions to independent trade unions and less censorship as long
as Poland remained a socialist, one-party state loyal to the Soviet Union.

The Soviets, however, were impatient, and demanded forceful action
should Kania fail to contain the "antisocialist elements." The conservative, septuagenarian Soviet leadership had left no doubt that they would
risk military intervention in Poland if the alternative was collapse of the
system. "The Soviet Union needs socialist Poland," said *Trybuna ludu* in
its commentary on Kania's visit to Moscow,[7] a reminder that the "bour-
geois path of development" before World War II ended in the destruction
of the Polish state by a coordinated Nazi-Soviet attack. In an apparent
warning to Poland, Leonid Zamyatin, head of the Soviet Central Committee's Department of International Information, made some very threatening remarks just two weeks after Kania's visit to Moscow. He stressed
that "elements hostile to Poland, including those in Poland itself, are trying to use the difficulties that have cropped up in order to undermine the
trust of the working class, the mass of the working people, in the leading
role of the PZPR [Polish United Workers' Party] as the vanguard of the
Polish society . . . Anti-socialist groups operating in Poland are in a certain way teaming up with external groups coming out against Socialist
Poland. Not the entire Polish working class has understood the complex-
ity of the situation and the whole danger arising to Socialist Poland."[8]

In particular, the Soviets feared Solidarity's idea of nonviolent struggle with communist totalitarianism, defined by *Literaturnaya gazeta* (5 November 1980) as "evolutionism." Because it was impossible to overthrow by force a Polish regime supported by the military might of Soviet Russia, the opposition selected a step-by-step, or evolutionary, process that would gradually alter the internal situation in Poland, as well as the balance of power in Europe. Solidarity, in the Soviet view, was nothing but a Trojan horse of "imperialism."

These remarks were a direct Soviet reaction to the Polish Supreme Court's 10 November decision to register the independent, self-governing Polish trade union and to approve its status, which had no reference to the leading role of the communist party. Solidarity's significant victory was ignored by the Soviet media, which instead decided to report on military maneuvers by Polish and Soviet forces. Polish television followed the Soviet lead, showing troop movements that were "strengthening . . . defense readiness."[9] A military solution of the Polish crisis loomed as Polish communist authority continued to weaken. The most ominous Soviet pronouncement came on 10 December. Addressing a conference of the party organization of the Moscow Military District, Soviet defense minister Marshal Dimitrii Ustinov accused the United States and West Germany of interfering in Poland's domestic affairs, and failed to mention that the Polish authorities could handle the situation alone.[10] A gloomy political atmosphere hung over Poland in expectation of an armed intervention by Soviet, East German, and Czechoslovak units.

The communist regimes of Eastern Europe joined Moscow in exerting strong pressure on Warsaw and Solidarity. The communist rulers of Czechoslovakia and East Germany, the most orthodox satellites of the Soviet Union, perceived Solidarity as a frontal attack on the external and internal security of socialism. The Polish crisis was simply the next attempt by "counterrevolutionary" forces to alter political order in a socialist country. After the failure of Czechoslovakia's "counterrevolution" in 1968, the West was trying to draw the Polish workers into a struggle against the communist party. Both Prague and East Berlin were afraid that the Polish workers' example would spread to their countries. The most precarious period of the crisis was between the U.S. presidential elections and the inauguration (5 November 1980 to 20 January 1981)—a relative vacuum of power in the West. In early December, Moscow ordered an unprecedented buildup of its forces along the Polish border; East Germany canceled military leaves and called up the reservists.[11]

Poland was in an uncomfortable strategic position, encircled on three sides by 64 Soviet divisions plus East German and Czech units. It was estimated that the Soviets needed an army of approximately one million men to overwhelm the 400,000-man Polish military, which is generally considered to be one of the best and most patriotic in Eastern Europe.[12] The invasion of Czechoslovakia in 1968 had involved 500,000 troops despite claims by the Czech government that the country would not resist the invaders.

The plan to invade Poland assumed that there would be a full-scale war. Soviet paratroops would be dropped on most of Poland's 60 airfields to secure safe landing for Soviet transport planes delivering troops, tanks, and armored personnel carriers for quick penetration of Poland's major cities. A Soviet naval attack on the Polish ports of Gdańsk, Gdynia, and Szczecin would neutralize the Polish navy and the merchant fleet. East German troops most likely would be used as "the anvil against which the hammer of the Russian Army would crush the Poles."[13]

The Poles were expected to resist. Depending on how loyal the top Polish commanders were to the Soviets, Polish resistance would either take the form of a Polish-Soviet war or be limited to localized opposition by relatively small groups of soldiers and armed civilians. Estimates of the duration of Polish resistance varied from a few weeks to several months. There was no doubt, however, that Poland would have been overrun eventually by the Soviets, who would then face the most difficult and economically expensive task—keeping the Poles under control.

Poland's determination to oppose the invasion deterred the Soviets, as did the impact that a war in Central Europe would have had on European détente and stability. Leaders of the European Community met in Luxembourg on 1–2 December, and issued a "robust" warning to Moscow, reminding the Soviets of the Helsinki accord, in which they had renounced "the use of threat of force." The Luxembourg communiqué also stated that "very serious consequences for the future of international relations in Europe and throughout the world" were likely to follow a Soviet invasion of Poland.[14]

Yet there was never any question regarding Soviet commitment to preserving Poland's pro-Soviet orientation. In 1956, Moscow recognized the necessity of tolerating a high degree of Polish nonconformity; but the collapse of a communist system would have a domino effect within the Soviet empire, including East Germany. The Soviets were not ready to admit the historical failure of communism, nor were they inclined to give up their imperial ambitions, even at the price of a world crisis.

Solidarity ignored this Soviet brinkmanship, confident that the Soviets, who just a year before had invaded Afghanistan, would avoid a prolonged military entanglement with the Polish nation. The union accepted the communist party leadership in principle. Thus Moscow had no reason to invade. Speaking for the union, Jacek Kuron characterized Soviet military preparations as a bluff. "The Soviet Union knows that a war would break out here if it invaded. Moscow does not want that and Poland does not want it either." Solidarity was not overstepping the limits of Soviet tolerance, according to Kuron, because "the leading role of the party means that the party has a monopoly situation in the army, the police, the orientation of foreign policy and in central government."[15]

Instead of "fraternal assistance," Moscow decided to give the Polish leadership another chance to put its house in order. On 5 December 1980, the Soviets called a special meeting of the Warsaw Pact countries; the Poles were given a chance to account for themselves and were allegedly granted another four weeks to end the crisis. According to a high-ranking East German official, it was a very unusual gathering, which included specialists on ideology and internal security as well as party chiefs, prime ministers, and foreign and defense ministers. The group decided that "the Polish Army could intervene first," and that only total anarchy would warrant external intervention.[16] Poland won some breathing space, plus new Soviet hard-currency credits worth $1.1 billion and $200 million worth of goods to be supplied in 1981.[17] Still, the Soviets continued preparations for a military invasion, keeping as many as 500,000 troops on 72-hour alert.[18]

Soviet relations with Poland continued to be restrained, but Moscow again expressed confidence in the Polish communist party's ability to overcome difficulties and bring the union under control. Warsaw's decision to call an emergency party congress was first seen by Moscow as a positive development. Preparations for this event were expected to mobilize the party and give it new momentum in its struggle with Solidarity. Official justification for the extraordinary congress was that the old leadership were not living up to the promises they had made, and that a thorough re-examination of the party's program and cadre policy was required.

From the military point of view, winter in Eastern Europe was most convenient for a full-scale invasion; spring rains would soften the soil and inhibit the movement of heavy equipment. While the Soviet military machine stood poised to attack Poland, Moscow's propaganda apparatus kept busy accusing Solidarity and the West of continuing attempts to take over political power in Poland. The Soviets were prepared to accept Solidarity as long as the union did not challenge the political primacy of the party and its alliance with Moscow. Technically, the existence of Solidarity as a labor union was not contradictory within the communist system. As the union became more militant, however, and as the party's control weakened, the Polish security apparatus became more provocative and tempted to act on its own. The country was drifting toward confrontation. The primary issue was no longer in what form the communist system could be preserved. Now Moscow and some Western states that had invested heavily in Poland in the 1970s began to fear that there was insufficient authority left to enforce any kind of order. The Soviet media began to question the Polish communist party's willingness to oppose Solidarity's political ambition. The PZPR was frequently compared to an onion with its layers being peeled off and only its core intact.

While the Polish leadership was under attack from Moscow for its weakness and tolerance of subversion, a small group of party members set up a pro-Soviet faction that became known as the Katowice Forum. In an open letter addressed to all members of the PZPR, they appealed for the "activization and consolidation" of the party so it could lead the struggle against the "forces hostile to socialism." The Polish workers, the letter continued, were "intercepted and subordinated" to the "counterrevolutionary" and "reactionary circles" of the West. All members of the party were asked to "block the way to these forces and mount a resolute struggle to disclose the true aims and intentions of the enemies of socialism in Poland." Finally, members of the Katowice Forum called for unity in the struggle for the socialist future of Poland.[19]

The emergence of the Katowice Forum was more than just another expression of the Soviet displeasure with the Polish leadership. It was a calculated move signaling Moscow's plan to establish an alternative center of power, which at any time could issue an "invitation" on behalf of the Polish workers to the Soviets to come in defense of the "gains of socialism in Poland." The Katowice Forum became an element in Soviet contingency planning, designed to create an outlet in Poland for criticism of the Polish communists. Should the Red Army invade, the political structure was ready to legitimize aggression and take over administrative functions. Moscow again applied a method used since World War II to take over smaller states. Preparing for the Sovietization of Poland in 1943, the Soviets had organized the so-called union of Polish patriots—the same technique used in 1968 before entering Czechoslovakia.

Only the Polish armed forces were exempt from Soviet criticism. Polish officers and enlisted men were frequently cited for their devotion to socialism and friendship with the Soviet Union. *Krasnaia zvezda,* the main publication of the Soviet Army, carried numerous reports on Soviet-Polish military exercises, stressing spontaneous cooperation and friendship among Polish and Soviet soldiers. Soviet analyses of the Polish situation implied that the working class might have been corrupted, but the disease had no ill effect on Polish servicemen. In effect, *Krasnaia zvezda* assumed that loyalty to socialism and "Soviet friendship, Soviet fraternity" precedes loyalty to one's country. "Socialism—and there is no other way" was supposedly the most popular slogan among the Polish soldiers, the defense of socialism being seen as the most "vital" and "honorable" duty.[20]

Without any reference to the national interest of the Polish people or Poland's two-hundred-year struggle for independence from imperial and Soviet Russia, *Krasnaia zvezda* deliberately falsified the nationalistic character of the Polish army, probably to create the notion that Polish troops would join the Soviets in suppressing Solidarity, which by late spring 1981 claimed more than ten million members. Soviet correspondents in Poland even went so far as to quote an army corporal as asking them to "pass our heartfelt thanks to the Soviet people for their economic and moral support and tell the soldiers of the Soviet armed forces that the Polish soldiers will always be with them in a united battle formation."[21]

In reality, the Soviets did not count on the Polish troops' loyalty to the Warsaw Pact. Momentum toward a Soviet military intervention built during the first half of 1981, when at least twenty divisions were kept on high alert in the western Soviet Union, East Germany, and Czechoslovakia. Soviet concern continued to grow as Warsaw seemed unable to govern without yielding to the union. Every confrontation between the Polish people and their government ended with a retreat by the communist party. Solidarity's "pressure" approach to the party, especially threats of a general strike, kept the party on the run and increasingly alarmed the Soviets. Solidarity became a genuine political opposition, representing more than 80 percent of the Polish work force, including 700,000 members of the PZPR.

The liberalizing trend affected rank-and-file party members, who began to question the basic principles of the party's Soviet-style democratic centralism. Democratization at the bottom of the party structure paralleled an acute power struggle at the top. Moscow's primary source of influence in Poland was disintegrating. Moscow reacted by adding two new themes to its analysis of the Polish situation. First, the Kremlin's disapproval of the Polish leadership became direct and personal. Attempts were made to discredit Kania and his associates. Second, the Soviet media stressed the international nature of the crisis by pointing to alleged "imperialist intervention" in Poland. In effect, Moscow invoked the doctrine of limited sovereignty in an attempt to provide justification for military intervention.[22]

Identifying Solidarity with counterrevolution indicated another shift in the Kremlin's policy toward Poland. As long as the expression of dissatisfaction with mistakes committed by the previous communist leadership in Poland was seen as legitimate—although "antisocialist elements" were trying to take advantage of the situation—compromise and reconciliation with the union was theoretically possible. Once the union was defined as a class enemy, however, an amicable solution was automatically ruled out. On 6 May 1981, *Literaturnaya gazeta* published the following: "A counterrevolutionary process is at work in the country and therefore appropriate methods ought to be used against it—i.e., the party must use all available means in the struggle against the counterrevolution."[23]

The Soviets frequently called for "a return to Marxism-Leninism" in 1981. Moscow strove to bring the outspoken Polish media under control and unite the conservative wing of the Polish communist party in an effort to replace Kania. Party liberalism, which was noted before the extraordinary ninth congress of the Polish United Workers' Party, was seen as an unrestrained growth of "revisionism and opportunism"—the result of the government's tolerance of private property and the influence of the Catholic church. Soviet attitudes had become orthodox and narrow-minded, revealing an impatience with the persistent instability in Poland. At the same time, the Soviets failed to realize that their interference with Poland's domestic affairs and the internal matters of the PZPR was one of the principal causes for the chaos.

The great pressure exerted by Moscow on Poland had relatively little effect on Solidarity and the party. In essence, it was unclear what Moscow was really trying to achieve, because the Soviet leadership had accepted the necessity of political and economic reforms in Poland but opposed the takeover of the Polish communist party by moderates bent on changes along democratic lines. Clearly, Moscow would like to see the party reverse its drift toward liberalization. However, only a democratically organized party could solve social disorders caused by strict adherence to democratic centralism. That basic operational principle deprives the party leadership in a Soviet-like state of the benefits of a second opinion, leaving mistakes uncorrected until their consequences are fatal to stability and, ultimately, to the legitimacy of the party.

Public criticism of a fraternal communist party was exceptional within the Soviet bloc, where secrecy is a standard operating procedure. Only when secret consultation and pressure proved fruitless would Moscow attack another communist party publicly. It tended to do so initially in the mass media; if such an indirect approach failed to intimidate the satellite party, the Central Committee of the Communist Party of the Soviet Union (CPSU) would then take a public stand. The Soviet invasions of Hungary in 1956 and of Czechoslovakia in 1968 indicated that the Soviet leadership's going public was the best evidence that quiet diplomacy had been unproductive.

Threatened by a nationwide strike, the Polish government publicly conceded that police were involved in the beating of union members at

Bydgoszcz, although the Soviet news agency Tass claimed that reports of the incident were fabricated by Solidarity. In addition, the Polish authorities agreed to a controversial meeting of intellectuals at Warsaw University, where numerous speakers discussed the failures of communist rule in Poland. The Kremlin wanted the Polish communist leadership to take a tough stand against the union, that is, to counterattack against Solidarity and liberals within the party. The Soviets were cornered; they had no influence on developments in Poland and were unsure of the consequences a military solution might have in Europe and how it might affect the popularity of communism throughout the world.

Under these circumstances, Moscow addressed a formal letter to the Polish Central Committee. The Soviet communists told the Poles that they had discussed "the mortal danger that now looms over the Polish people's revolutionary achievements," and that "unfortunately, these friendly warnings . . . were not taken into account and were even ignored." The CPSU Central Committee letter asserted that "continual concessions to antisocialist forces and their demands have led to a situation in which the PZPR has been falling back step by step under the pressure of internal counterrevolution, which has been supported by imperialist foreign centers of diversion."

The entire country, in the Soviet view, was falling prey to "a criminal plot against people's power . . . [that] also constitutes a threat to the very existence of an independent Polish state." Instead of taking the initiative in this struggle against "imperialist" influence in Poland, the Soviets noted that the Polish communist party had become confused and even neglected to "protect its cadres from enemy attacks." In reference to the forthcoming PZPR congress, the Soviet leadership expressed its displeasures with the idea of multiple candidacies and secret-ballot election of party delegates, many of whom were "openly preaching opportunist viewpoints." Democratization within the party, the Soviet letter stated, created a situation in which "experienced activists entirely devoted to the party and with irreproachable reputations and morals are being passed over."

Finally, the letter indicated a Soviet willingness to give the Polish leadership one more chance "of avoiding the worst and averting a national disaster." Reiterating the Brezhnev Doctrine, the Soviet leadership claimed that should the Polish communists fail to bring their country back to the Soviet line, "we will not permit any attack on socialist Poland and will not abandon a fraternal country in misfortune."[24]

The struggle for control of the Polish communist party had become the Soviets' top issue. They were afraid that the congress would eliminate most hard-liners from the Polish leadership, leaving the party even more vulnerable to Solidarity. The Soviet strategy for the Polish crisis called for consolidating the communist authority in Poland before attacking Solidarity. The Soviet letter was an explicit request to make personnel changes in Poland's top leadership. In effect, however, the letter was entirely counterproductive. The first secretary of the PZPR, Stanisław Kania, called an emergency Central Committee meeting, which unified the Polish party around his leadership just five weeks before the congress. Moscow's saber-rattling approach backfired again, shifting the whole party to the left. To make this point clearer and stronger, Polish radio announced that the "comrades in uniform" supported the party line followed by Kania and General Wojciech Jaruzelski, because both of them were mentioned in the Soviet letter. The message to Moscow was that more than 140 military delegates to the congress and the entire Polish armed forces were firmly on Kania's side. The Soviet leaders were being told that if they decided to use force against Poland, they would face organized resistance.

The Soviet letter, which was in effect a form of ultimatum informing the Poles that the option for intervention remained open, was followed by a more subtle diplomatic initiative. In early July, less than two weeks before the congress, Andrei Gromyko, who at that time was a member of the CPSU Central Committee Politburo and the Soviet foreign minister, arrived in Warsaw for a working visit. His discussion with the Polish leadership must have included Warsaw's determination to proceed with the reform program, which in Moscow appeared subversive to the leading role of the party; with the personnel changes in the Polish Politburo, the Soviets openly expressing a preference for Stefan Olszowski, a hard-liner with good connections in Moscow; and with the congress, which Gromyko wanted to postpone.[25]

Proposed changes to the party status in Poland were of particular concern for the Soviets. In addition to secret-ballot elections, the Poles intended to limit the number of terms in office an individual could serve, to allow mandates to be withdrawn for incompetence or corruption, and to hold the Politburo accountable to the Central Committee. These changes could permanently alter the centralized nature of the communist party, which ensured that all decisions were made at the top and were carried out by the lower units. A group of radical Polish reformers, the "horizontalists," envisioned both a complete departure from Leninism and a party restructured according to genuine democratic principles. These changes would break new ground in Eastern Europe and could affect other ruling parties.

Despite the Soviets' concern, however, the tide of Polish reforms could not be halted. The Kremlin allowed the Polish communists to have their extraordinary congress and move forward with reforms. After all, the central party apparatus was still firmly in control. Continuing Soviet pressure had destabilized the party, and a victory for the hard-liners could trigger popular revolt. The communiqué that ended Gromyko's visit was vague, but implied that Moscow would tolerate substantial changes in Poland, providing that the alliance with Moscow and "common ideology" were left intact.[26]

The net result of Soviet pressure on Poland was a sense of realism for both the party and the opposition. The entire nation understood how insecure, arrogant, and prone to overreact the Soviets were, and how they mechanically assumed that any attempt to reform the petrified system was a manifestation of foreign subversion. The Soviet leaders had very little understanding and no sympathy for the Polish workers, who were seen as no more than an obstacle to Soviet global ambitions.

Soviet behavior before the Polish party congress was politically destructive, because it fueled both ideological and regional intraparty divisions. Instead of contributing to PZPR unity and cohesion, the Soviets undermined its authority by presenting the party as a Soviet puppet whose loyalty to the Warsaw Pact should come first. The Soviets' intimidation of Poland brought to mind the worst memories of partitions and the 1939 Nazi-Soviet pact. Most Poles refused to be humiliated again, even if such refusal risked another defeat. Nothing was so likely to induce in the Poles a stubborn, die-hard attitude as an attempt to coerce them with a Russian or German threat. To rebel against oppression is considered a moral duty by the Poles, who are not necessarily looking for immediate results but are more inclined to consider the historical perspective and the impact their actions might have upon future generations.

The aging Soviet leadership appeared to be unaware of the contradiction between an antiquated ideology, economic system, and political authority on the one hand, and the realities of socioeconomic life on the other. This lack of awareness contributed to Moscow's misconceptions about Polish events. The Polish phenomenon of 1980–81 was, to some extent, a premature *glasnost'*—a reaction against the self-serving, hypocritical bureaucracy of the Brezhnev regime. It was an attempt to find a new social equilibrium in which the authorities would be more sensitive to popular pressures and more competent in handling economic matters. The Polish communist system was crippled by the excesses of democratic centralism, which suffocated constructive criticism within the party. Poland was expected to pay for the consequences of irrational policies formulated in a vacuum by ignorant party hacks who were oblivious to professional opinion. Brezhnev lived long enough to see only the beginning of fundamental changes in the communist system—changes that he confused with a counterrevolution. He did not understand that the purpose of Solidarity's political struggle with the regime was to reform the regime, not replace it. The union was not against socialism, rather, it was in favor of a more democratic and pragmatic socialism that would be compatible both with national aspirations and with the Soviet guidelines for a socialist state.

The emergency party congress did not liquidate Polish communism, as Moscow feared. Nevertheless, it was vastly different from typical Soviet-bloc party congresses, which are well orchestrated and follow plans precisely. The new Polish party leadership was elected by secret ballot after much maneuvering by the delegates. Stanisław Kania was re-elected as the party's first secretary by majority vote. Though this was a victory for the moderates, pro-Soviet hard-liners preserved their influence at all levels of the communist hierarchy. New rules adopted by the congress included a two-term (or ten-year) limit in office, and the right to recall incompetent officials. These changes did not alter the centralized character of the party, however. While Western observers focused their attention on the democratic features of the congress, Moscow was quick to notice that the "revisionist" aspects were of marginal importance.[27] The congress strongly endorsed the principles of democratic socialism and the leading role of the party. In addition, First Secretary Kania stated that "the congress gives full assurance that this party and this country will remain allies of the Soviet Union and the socialist community." He also said that "all attempts at undermining the Marxist character of the congress met with a resolute rebuff."[28]

Although the ninth extraordinary party congress was an unusual event, it was not very productive, because intraparty matters took priority over economic reforms and political stability. The party was reformed and mobilized without addressing the key social and economic issues. The impression was given that the party had taken action to normalize the domestic situation; in reality, the impasse between the authorities and the union was left unresolved. Both organizations rapidly searched for new ways to increase their political power in preparation for a final showdown. Solidarity opted for political activism and more radical programs, whereas the party emphasized the growing role of the armed forces.

Gen. Wojciech Jaruzelski, Poland's prime minister since February 1981, had become the number two man in the ruling Politburo. He used his power to consolidate the regime by placing generals in key ministerial positions such as internal affairs, security, energy, and administration. The army has traditionally enjoyed respect from the Poles; Jaruzelski's actions suggested that a decisive political step was to follow. In early August 1981, Kania and Jaruzelski went to the Crimea and briefed Brezhnev about the Polish situation. It is possible that the decision to impose martial law was made there, since the Soviets subsequently ceased their attacks on the Polish authorities and focused on the allegedly antisocialist, anti-Soviet, and counterrevolutionary character of the union, which they accused of being subservient to "Western imperialism." A military solution to the Polish crisis was agreed upon; under the approved plan the blood was to be let by Poles while the Soviet leaders pretended that their hands were clean.

In addition to political and military means, Moscow used its economic weapons to exert pressure on Poland. Generally, Poles were described to Soviet citizens as ungrateful for their liberation from the Nazis and for the Soviets' enormous economic assistance. In fact, within the first year of the Polish crisis, Moscow had granted Poland loans exceeding $4 billion, including hard-currency credits of about $1 billion for purchasing some indispensable Western goods. Poland, however, was unable to fulfill its export obligations to the Soviets, and in September 1981 Moscow implied that it would insist on balanced trade with Poland in 1982. Instead of the planned 4.4 billion rubles' worth of imports from the Soviet Union, Poland's imports would be reduced to 2.7 billion rubles—the amount of Polish exports to the Soviet Union. Stating the Soviet position, Stefan Olszowski, a conservative member of the Polish Politburo, said that "the Soviet Union can do without Polish supplies, but Poland cannot do without Russian supplies." He added that the Poles were like "a little boy sitting on a branch of a tree, holding on to it with one hand and cutting it off with the other."[29]

Olszowski's statement was correct in the sense that it reflected the political strategy adopted by the regime in dealing with Solidarity. Honest implementation of the August 1980 accord between the Polish government and the union would have terminated the communist monopoly of power in Poland. Some form of coalition incorporating the regime, the Catholic church, and the union would have to be established to fill the power vacuum left by the disintegrating communist order. To avoid this necessity, in fall 1981 the regime adopted a policy of provocation toward Solidarity, deliberately encouraging more radical elements to dominate the union. Thus the regime scrupulously followed cynical Leninist tactics ("the worse the better") that paralyzed all efforts to address the painful economic crisis. The regime accused the union of deliberately wrecking the 1981 accord and pushing the nation toward economic and political disaster.

On 18 October 1981, the Central Committee removed Stanisław Kania from the post of first secretary and replaced him with General Jaruzelski, who was already prime minister and minister of defense. The Polish regime was thus completely militarized. The party could no longer be trusted; one-third of its members joined Solidarity and another one-third left the party altogether. General Jaruzelski formed a core of political power dominated by army and internal security generals. On 4 November, the new party chief met with Solidarity leader Lech Wałęsa and Archbishop Glemp. He demanded the immediate suspension of strikes and agreed to open talks on forming a Front of National Unity. These steps were intended to portray the regime as conciliatory and eager to compromise. At the same time, however, Jaruzelski indicated that he would ask the Sejm to grant him the authority to declare a state of emergency. The regime was no longer interested in negotiations with the union; intensive preparations were under way for a military takeover that would eliminate the opposition and restore amicable relations with the Soviet Union. Marshal Kulikov, commander of the Warsaw Pact forces, was sent to Poland to oversee Jaruzelski's attack on the Polish nation, which took place on Saturday the night of 12 December 1981.

General Jaruzelski's coup, intended to restore pro-Soviet order in Poland, was greeted with approval in the Soviet press. Several articles published in *Pravda* stressed that martial law prevented "internationalization" of the Polish problem, which, the Soviet sources emphasized, was settled by the Poles themselves without any outside involvement. The Polish people, according to Moscow, averted an imminent anticommunist coup and re-established law and public order. The United States and other NATO countries were blamed for Poland's attempted "counterrevolution." The official Soviet view was expressed in a *Pravda* article signed by Aleksey Petrov, who described the implementation of martial law as a historical victory of the Polish nation against the forces of imperialism and against U.S. president Ronald Reagan's anticommunist crusade. The Soviets condemned the U.S. administration for inciting the Poles to undermine the socialist community of nations, "to introduce a split in the socialist world, and, at the same time, to shake the whole existing system of international relations." Poland, in the Soviet view, was to be a springboard for penetrating the communist bloc and eventually altering the post–World War II balance of power—to change the correlation of forces in the world. *Pravda* also alleged that the United States violated the principle of "equality and equal security" by "confusing the Polish People's Republic with California and Texas." Solidarity, according to Moscow, was not the first independent trade union in Eastern Europe, but rather a Western scheme to deprive the Soviet Union of superpower status.[30]

The Polish government admitted only that the Soviet Union had advance knowledge of the imposition of martial law.[31] In fact, not only were the Soviet leaders informed about Jaruzelski's coup, it was their pressure that persuaded the Polish government to undertake the destruction of Solidarity. In an interview in the April 1987 Paris *Kultura,* Col. Ryszard

Kukliński, a member of the General Staff of the Polish Army who defected to the West on 8 November 1981, reported that the decision to impose martial law in Poland was made under direct Soviet pressure. The Polish regime was warned that if the Polish military and police forces failed to destroy Solidarity, Poland would be invaded by Soviet, Czechoslovakian, and East German forces. The Soviets insisted on an early confrontation with the union and, in effect, with the entire Polish nation. They believed that counterrevolution should be exterminated regardless of the price, and that its leaders should be killed or deported to the Soviet Union. The Kania-Jaruzelski leadership, according to Colonel Kuklinski, merely argued that outside intervention was too costly and reassured Moscow that it was unnecessary, since the regime had the ability to crush the workers. Because Moscow and Warsaw agreed that Solidarity must be crushed, the Polish authorities never considered establishing a united front with the union to resist Soviet intimidation—as Polish leader Władysław Gomułka did in October 1956 when he consolidated the entire nation, mobilized Polish troops, and dissuaded Nikita Khrushchev from invading Poland. The Kania-Jaruzelski regime agreed with Moscow that Solidarity was too dangerous to communism to be allowed to survive; the only disagreement involved the method of execution.

Whereas the Soviets favored a radical solution similar to their actions in Hungary and Czechoslovakia, Polish communists preferred a gradual strategy of attrition that would wear down Polish society, outmaneuver Solidarity, and eventually decapitate the union with one swift blow. It is very likely that General Jaruzelski was motivated by a genuine concern for Poland's fate, but it must be noted that a Soviet invasion could have included major personnel changes in Warsaw. Self-interest was not absent from his calculations. A group of communist hard-liners headed by Stefan Olszowski and certainly supported by Moscow had already stated its intention to take over political power if General Jaruzelski continued to procrastinate or failed to impose martial law. The assault on Solidarity was executed at night, 12–13 December, when internal security forces, supported by military units acting as Soviet proxies, ended sixteen months of freedom. Marshal Viktor Kulikov arrived in Warsaw three days before the attack on Solidarity and personally supervised the operation. Nevertheless, Moscow proclaimed that the military solution was purely an internal decision made by a sovereign state.

With the military takeover of Poland complete, official Soviet sources published allegations that Solidarity was supported by a Western counter-revolutionary organization, and that a terrorist group was preparing a violent overthrow of the communist government. The Soviet press carried sensational, but unsubstantiated, reports on terrorist activities in Poland, frequently citing undocumented numbers of assassinated policemen, workers, and even children. Discoveries were reported of weapons, ammunition, and toxic agents stored by Solidarity in preparation for armed resistance.[32]

The Soviets portrayed Solidarity in the most negative manner, to make the idea of an independent union unattractive to workers in other East European states. The attempt to organize workers outside of the official structure was equated with terrorism. Another purpose of this postmortem anti-Solidarity campaign was to influence General Jaruzelski's handling of the arrested activists. Moscow asked for decisive steps, including executions for criminal acts attributed to Solidarity members. Martial law resulted in relatively little violence; fewer than twenty people were killed during the first few days after the attack. Moreover, the military regime proclaimed its intention to seek a national reconciliation with the opposition. Meanwhile, the Sejm was asked to set up a state tribunal to determine the guilt of the party leadership responsible for the economic crisis during the late 1970s.[33]

The Soviet press also praised the contributions of the Polish communist party in liberating the Polish workers from the Nazi occupation and "capitalist exploitation." In connection with the 40th anniversary of the Polish United Workers' Party, *Pravda* wrote of the "glorious traditions of the previous generations of proletarian revolutionaries" in Poland, stressing their ability to solve the enormous, complex tasks facing them and to "put an end to the counterrevolutionary attempts to push the country off the socialist path which has been chosen by the people."[34] The Soviet dailies attributed Solidarity's destruction to the party, rather than the military, to minimize embarrassment and dissuade Jaruzelski from dissolving the most unpopular organization in Poland.

The liberal wing of the party recommended that the military leaders dissolve the party and replace it with a coalition of communists, Catholics, and socialists, but this was never seriously considered. Such a solution to social tensions in a Soviet-bloc country would be unwelcome in Moscow; it would be as threatening to the communist order as an independent trade union. Martial law was imposed in Poland to restore socialism rather than replace it with a military or semidemocratic system. This point was discussed during the first official meeting between high-ranking Soviet and Polish leaders after the military takeover. Jósef Czyrek—a member of the Politburo, and Poland's foreign minister—went to Moscow on 10–12 January 1982 to meet with his Soviet counterpart, Andrei Gromyko, and with Mikhail Suslov, a member of the Soviet Politburo and secretary of the Soviet Central Committee. Their joint communiqué reaffirmed Warsaw's commitment to the "principles of Marxism-Leninism . . . [and] friendship, cooperation, and mutual assistance."[35]

It is surprising that, immediately after being coerced by Moscow to take military action against their own nation, the Polish leaders were forced to make public oaths of loyalty to the Soviet Union. It should be noted, however, that the Soviets were never comfortable with General Jaruzelski's nationalistic overtones and political restraint. They must have feared that if the party lost its leading role, the Polish military might be reluctant to transfer authority back to the Politburo. In fact, the party had to wait some time for its authority to be reinstated; this occurred only after Jaruzelski had appointed his own men to key positions in the Secretariat, Politburo, and Central Committee. Once Jaruzelski had accumulated such enormous power, the Soviets feared that he might try to win popularity at home by means of a Tito-like contempt for Moscow.

The Poles were compelled to harmonize their foreign policy with Moscow's, explicitly accusing the United States of imperialism, militarism, and a policy of brute force and diktat. When pressed by Moscow, the regime attacked Washington for its alleged interference in Poland's internal affairs, and even accused the United States of directly violating the United Nations Charter and the basic principles of state-to-state relations.

Poland was rapidly losing its autonomy and falling entirely into line with Soviet foreign policy, which was characterized by an unusually high level of hostility toward the United States. By blaming the Reagan administration for undermining the foundation of European security and cooperation, Warsaw joined Moscow in its attempt to divide the NATO countries and shift attention from Polish events to such issues as the limitation of nuclear forces in Europe. With Moscow, General Jaruzelski's military regime attempted to intimidate Western Europe into focusing on the threat of nuclear war, rather than on human rights issues in Poland. As in previous Soviet invasions against its satellites, Moscow's position was that it had the exclusive right to decide Eastern European political issues; and that Western concerns about East European nations violated the principles of equality and equal security.

By joining the Soviet Union in its attacks on the United States and in its systematic distortion of reality, the Polish government reduced itself to a Soviet puppet, echoing Moscow's policies and statements of foreign policy. Warsaw had won international prestige in the 1970s because Poland acted as an independent partner of the Soviet Union, making its own significant contribution to the peace process in Europe. Perhaps unavoidably under the circumstances, Poland's full identification with Moscow was self-defeating. It discredited Poland in Western eyes and rendered Warsaw useless as a go-between with Moscow. Poland ceased to exist as an actor on the European diplomatic stage. The Polish regime lost its sense of reality and moderation; the 11 January NATO declaration condemning the imposition of martial law in Poland was criticized as Western interference in Polish internal affairs, while the Soviet Union was praised for respecting the principle of self-determination.

CHAPTER TWO

Restoration of the Status Quo

Following the military takeover of Poland, Soviet matters began to dominate Warsaw's international activities. Various Soviet delegations visited Poland for talks with members of the Polish Politburo, the Polish government, and the state planning commission. Great progress in restoring relations with the Soviet Union became the main theme of Polish media reports. Stories about large food consignments from the East and progress toward full reintegration into the Soviet commonwealth of nations became the mainstay of the media. Soviet relief, the Polish authorities argued, helped Poland avoid the tragedy that U.S. economic restrictions would have inflicted on Poland. Deliveries of Soviet crude oil and raw materials for Polish industry arrested the economic crisis, according to Warsaw, and gave a significant boost to the stabilization of Poland's economy.

In fact, the Polish authorities assumed that economic cooperation with the Soviet Union, plus the "normal work rhythm," could do much more for the Polish economy than a radical restructuring of the nation's economic system. The authorities had never denied the necessity of economic reforms, but economic stabilization now received top priority. The Warsaw regime subscribed to the old Soviet position that more work, rather than economic reforms, would solve Poland's problems. With Solidarity dispersed and its leaders in prison, the Soviet Union quickly managed to reassert its dominant position in Poland.

Normalizing Polish-Soviet relations during the first months of martial law was not only a necessity for Jaruzelski, but an opportunity to regain Poland's number two position, after the Soviet Union, within the Eastern bloc. Solidarity's legal existence had undermined Poland's standing among the members of the Warsaw Pact. Poland had acquired a reputation as the weak link in the international socialist system. Warsaw feared the consequences of being displaced by much smaller countries, such as Czechoslovakia or East Germany. Poland's demotion to a secondary position in the Warsaw Pact strengthened the most orthodox and militaristic regimes in the Soviet bloc and enhanced the positions of the most pro-Soviet and conservative elements in Poland. There was a danger that neo-Stalinism would lead to internal violence and exacerbate the socioeconomic crisis, raising the prospect of a Soviet invasion. General Jaruzelski tried to prevent this by imposing martial law.

Jaruzelski's brief visit to Moscow on 1–2 March 1982 symbolized Poland's position as the most important Soviet ally. Stressing form rather than substance, General Jaruzelski's hyperbolically ceremonial visit reaffirmed his personal leadership and Poland's healthy ideological recovery within the Soviet bloc. Similar visits to other East European capitals established personal contacts with other Warsaw Pact leaders. Dwelling on Jaruzelski's Moscow visit, *Novo vremyé* congratulated the Polish leadership for "restoring a Leninist work style, stepping up activity at enterprises and going among the masses." The article emphasized that "the Soviet Union and Poland expressed their unswerving determination to continue to act harmoniously and cohesively in the international arena," to indicate that Soviet-bloc unity was restored.[1]

Despite Moscow's blessing of General Jaruzelski and his policies, which was delivered personally by Leonid Brezhnev, many Soviet leaders continued to express displeasure with the way Poland was governed. In an article published in the February 1982 issue of the ideological journal *Voprosy istorii KPSS*, Konstantin Chernenko, a member of the Soviet Secretariat and Politburo, harshly criticized the Polish communists for tampering with the leading role of the party. Referring indirectly to Poland, Chernenko wrote that the ruling communist parties "must confirm every day and with their every decision their right to lead the country, otherwise, as the harsh lessons of recent years have shown, the political situation can reach a crisis."

General Jaruzelski was accepted in Moscow, but his relatively conciliatory policies were of great concern in the Kremlin, which was apprehensive about the Polish opposition's ability to organize underground. Initially, the union was merely suspended, and many expected that for the sake of national reconciliation the military regime would allow Solidarity to return to public life, provided that it confined itself to trade union activities and accepted the leadership of the communist party. Moscow feared that General Jaruzelski might now decide to experiment with pluralism to break the political and economic deadlock in Poland. Thus martial law did not end Poland's crisis.

The Soviets' uneasiness about Poland's future manifested itself in mid-May, when Konstantin Rusakov, a secretary of the Central Committee made a surprise visit to Warsaw, preceded by demonstrative Soviet–Polish–East German military maneuvers dubbed "Friendship '82." Rusakov publicly expressed Soviet opposition to the planned second visit to Poland by Pope John Paul II in summer 1982. How far the new Polish regime would accommodate political aspirations in a full-scale dialogue with the nation was unclear. Moscow continued to press for a solution that would completely liquidate Solidarity and restore the leading role of the communist party. Soviet economic aid, which was critical for Poland's economic survival, was contingent on Jaruzelski's enforcement of more repressive policies. The Polish authorities, however, attempted to balance the Soviet preference for tough measures with domestic demands for less repressive policies, once again trying to avoid provoking the Soviets or inciting the Poles to violent clashes with the authorities. Soviet reports on the Polish situation in 1982 usually contained contradictory analyses: on one hand, the situation was becoming more stable and "normal"; on the other hand, the "counterrevolutionary" danger for Poland was not over.

Another major show of military force was staged in late August 1982, during the second anniversary of the Gdańsk agreement. Soviet and Polish troops were made highly visible just outside Warsaw, to deter any possibility of public protest.[2] Several days before, General Jaruzelski had visited Leonid Brezhnev in the Crimea to give him a progress report on the Polish situation and to ask for a continuation of Soviet aid. It was probably at this meeting that the decision to disband Solidarity was made. The communiqué issued by the Polish Politburo stated that the Soviet Union and Poland achieved "complete unity—expressed in the talks—of stances and views," and concluded that Solidarity represented "the forces interested in destabilization" and that the union's activities were "inspired and actively supported by the subversive foreign centers." Finally, the Politburo noted with satisfaction that the Soviets approved the normalization policies followed by General Jaruzelski. For this reason, Poland received the personal "assurance of Leonid Brezhnev . . . that the Soviet Union will continue to give Poland all possible aid for emerging from the crisis situation."[3]

The Soviets successfully used their economic leverage to dictate internal policies in Poland. Western economic sanctions imposed in response to Poland's martial law threw the Poles into the arms of the Soviet Union. With the continuing economic crisis and the underground opposition, Jaruzelski was losing the freedom of movement that the declaration of martial law had provided. He was forced to recast the party according to Moscow-oriented principles and to take a more severe approach to the opposition. Relations between Poland and the Soviet Union began to resemble patterns followed under Stalin. Soviet influence was strong in Poland's top political and military levels from the outset; but soon Soviet security officials and bureaucrats representing various economic branches began to penetrate the regional and even the local levels of authority in Poland.

The Soviet influence was to be consolidated by supplementing links between the two communist parties with cooperation in all socioeconomic spheres. The Polish economy was gradually integrated into the Soviet economic system. Some branches of the national economy, notably the electronics industry, were entirely subordinated to Soviet control through bilateral agreements. Poland's traditionally independent armed forces were subjected to very close Soviet control; Soviet military representatives established a permanent presence at all major Polish garrisons. In addition, Poland's security forces became closely linked with, and penetrated by, KGB representatives providing training and supervision for the pacification of Poland. The Warsaw regime began to copy Soviet domestic policies, particularly the new educational policy geared to increasing the familiarity and acceptance of communist ideas. One year after martial law was imposed, a pattern of Sovietization similar to that practiced in Stalin's time began to emerge. The authorities intended to suppress all democratic aspirations and establish a coercive, efficient totalitarian state unquestioningly loyal to Moscow.

As the political grip on Polish society tightened and the nation's will to resist weakened, Soviet control assumed a less visible character, focusing on building an extensive network of economic ties. Gradually, Poland's economic dependence on Moscow assumed new forms, including agreements on specialization and cooperation, on joint ventures, on scientific and technical research, and on the supply of raw materials. Unpopular and deprived of Western credits, Poland's military regime emphasized political priorities rather than economic necessities. The regime opened the door for Soviet penetration of Poland's public economic sector, fully aware that relations with the Soviets were acquiring traits of colonial exploitation. Economic reforms were originally supposed to end central planning and establish private enterprise and financing. In fact, only a new facade was placed on the old system of administrative command.

Geographically reorienting the Polish economy, which during the previous decade had balanced trade within the Soviet bloc with Western trade, was an easy short-term substitute for a politically inconvenient restructuring of the economy. The Jaruzelski regime's trump argument was that the increased ties between the Soviet and Polish economies were the key to a swift resolution of Poland's economic difficulties. Warsaw described the Soviet Union as a stable partner, supplying goods that were indispensable for Polish industry and the nation. On a scale and intensity unknown in Poland since Stalinism, the Polish authorities affirmed their eternal loyalty, unprecedented altruism, and eagerness to increase economic ties with the Soviets. Warsaw became merely a tool of Soviet foreign policy.

Almost daily attacks on Western states in the Polish press, especially against the United States, were often tougher ideologically than Soviet pronouncements. The Reagan administration in particular was repeatedly accused of neocolonialism, of following a dangerous policy of imperialism, and of attempting to use Poland as a pawn in Reagan's global assault on the Soviet Union. The indiscriminate fervor of Polish propaganda against the United States was most painfully evident after the Soviet downing of a Korean commercial airliner in September 1983. *Trybuna ludu* wrote that the entire incident was a U.S. provocation "for the benefit of forces that do not want accord, are striving to achieve military superiority over the socialist world, and are driving the world toward a confrontation."[4]

The Soviets were filling the vacuum left when Western economic sanctions were imposed on the military regime. Isolated from the West, most Poles saw Jaruzelski's regime as the guardian of Soviet hegemony. The Soviets transformed their economic assistance, calculated by various sources to reach $5 billion during 1980–83, into political dividends. During the European détente of the 1970s, Poland had emerged from the excessive dependence on Moscow that resulted from the unsettled international status of the country's western border. These gains were all wasted by Jaruzelski's military dictatorship. The Soviet Union's self-serving exaggeration of its role as the defender of Poland's sovereignty blinded General Jaruzelski and his colleagues to the fact that the coercive re-Sovietization of Poland had just the opposite result. Martial law divided and demoralized Polish society. The regime, determined to survive even without popular consensus, became vulnerable to Soviet pressure.

Thus for all practical purposes, Jaruzelski's politics had almost the same effect as an overt Soviet military intervention. Step-by-step, Poland's relative independence vanished. Every successful police action was at the expense of national independence. Regardless of how brutal the regime's official actions were, and to what extent domestic law and international treaties were contravened, Moscow insisted on more determination in the struggle against the opposition. Jaruzelski's successes, which were measured in the numbers of people imprisoned and social organizations dissolved, were actually testimonies of political weakness; but they were welcomed in Moscow, which saw them as signs of the Polish regime's unconditional loyalty to the Kremlin.

Violations of basic human rights, including assassination and imprisonment, became notorious practices during the first three years of military rule. They were strongly condemned in a U.N. resolution based on the report on the situation in Poland written by Hugo Gobbi, an under secretary-general.[5] As was expected, Warsaw strongly rejected both the report and the resolution, invoking the senseless argument that they constituted an illegal interference in Poland's internal affairs. The resolution was called "invalid, politically harmful and morally two-faced," and termed a U.S. fabrication.[6] Poland's international prestige was at its lowest since World War II. General Jaruzelski's regime served at the pleasure of Moscow.

It was a happy coincidence for the Poles that during the most critical years of martial law politics, the Soviet Union itself was immobilized owing to problems with the succession of its top leaders. Brezhnev's death in November 1982, followed by Iurii Andropov's brief term as general secretary (at least half of which was spent in the hospital), reduced Soviet pressure on Jaruzelski. Moreover, Andropov, unlike Brezhnev, fully understood the urgency of communist reform, and he gave Jaruzelski more freedom to appease Polish society. Andropov's approach to the Soviet empire permitted ideological compromise and the recognition of local peculiarities. The Soviet Union under Andropov had much more tolerance for Jaruzelski's "carrots and sticks" policy of dealing with the internal opposition.

Nevertheless, Andropov's personal preferences did not stop other Soviet leaders from expressing their dissatisfaction with a process of normalization that they saw as too lenient to deter political activists from challenging the authorities. Another very undesirable development, in the Soviet view, was Jaruzelski's strengthening of the political role of the military rather than restoring the power of the party leadership.

Unable to influence General Jaruzelski through internal party channels, Moscow criticized Mieczysław Rakowski. Formerly the editor of *Polityka*, at that time he was deputy prime minister and one of Jaruzelski's closest aides. On 6 May 1983, the Soviet periodical *Novo vremyé* carried an unprecedented attack against *Polityka*: an article by Andrei Ryzhov entitled, "When People Lose Their Bearings: On Some Pages in the Warsaw Weekly *Polityka.*" Ryzhov wrote that after sixteen months of "frontal counterrevolutionary onslaught" during the legal existence of Solidarity, martial law was a positive development, but that the cause of socialism was not secure because the counterrevolutionary elements continued to act. Proclaiming martial law and outlawing Solidarity were supposed to restore the monolithic communist system; instead, Ryzhov charged, official sources in Poland publicly advocated the pluralistic political perspective. One of *Polityka*'s chief political analysts was quoted as saying, "It is necessary once and for all to proclaim Poland to be a land of pluralism of world outlook and political pluralism."

Ryzhov went on to criticize the Polish intellectual and political leadership because it apologized for Solidarity and because it credited the union with "good will and the noblest motives not only among the many millions of ordinary members of the movement, but among its leadership too." Ryzhov wrote that the Poles went so far as to equate Solidarity with the slave uprisings in ancient Rome, and to compare Lech Wałęsa with Spartacus; the communist party, in contrast, was seen as an example of Marxism's bankruptcy because, according to *Polityka*, "Present-day Marxism does not devote enough attention to . . . the laws governing the spontaneous, elemental movement of the masses." The Polish view on the leading role of the party, continued Ryzhov's article, assumed that Marxism-Leninism had lost its creative potential and that the party should renounce its leading role in society. Rakowski was quoted as saying, "The party has fallen apart and because it is bankrupt, intellectually and politically, it is incapable of organizing society or leading the country out of catastrophe, and still less of defending the state."

Ryzhov next dealt with the geopolitical factor and its impact on Poland's internal political system. He wrote that socialism in Poland was not seen as a product of the objective laws of historical development; rather, according to the deputy chief editor of *Polityka*, "Our geopolitical location forces us to follow some kind of socialist path of development and . . . every revolt that violates that status is doomed to defeat. The only way out of this situation is to reconcile ourselves to destiny, to the system, and at the same time to gamble on perfecting it and reforming it in general."

The Poles saw themselves as victims of the Yalta and Potsdam conferences; but decisions made in Yalta should be regarded as eternal. *Polityka* was quoted again: "You do not have to be a Marxist or a specialist in dialectics to see that history is constant movement, that its mills grind slowly but inevitably and that the Vienna and Versailles treaties disintegrated although those who signed them believed they were decreeing the order for eternity."

Speaking for the Soviet authorities, Ryzhov's article accused the Poles of openly challenging the Soviet system, and of claiming that the system had not been voluntarily chosen but imposed on Poland by the military results of World War II. It is significant to note how deeply distrustful the Kremlin was toward the Polish regime and its long-term goal of shielding the Polish nation from the consequences of Soviet domination. In effect, the Soviets claimed to know that the Poles have never been inspired by Marxism-Leninism, and that their friendship with the Soviet Union had been motivated by their survival instinct rather than by genuine ideological or ethnic commonality of interests. Without actually using the term, the Soviets accused Poland of becoming the "Judas of socialism," just as in the previous century, when Poland was forcefully incorporated into the tsarist variant of the Russian empire, it was commonly referred to as the "Judas of Slavdom."

The article reflected the Russians' deep-seated, historical distrust of the Poles, who were seen as merely pretending to be communists and friends of Moscow. Martial law had failed to bridge Poland's political cleavage, and the underground Solidarity had not abandoned its political hopes. Moscow discovered that the opposition had changed its tactics, now planning to alter Poland's political system gradually; yet Jaruzelski's military regime had not changed its tactics to counter the opposition's long-term reorientation. The first key step toward an eventual Western-style democracy was to be the implementation of socialist pluralism. The Soviets faced a prolonged, costly, and embarrassing struggle in Poland, with the political forces of the opposition dispersed across the entire socioeconomic spectrum and using both illegal and legal means to change the framework of the socialist system. The leaders of the outlawed union did not relent, and the Polish regime adopted a policy of appeasement (by Soviet standards) toward the opposition, at the expense of vigorous ideological struggle.

The *Novo vremyé* attack on *Polityka* indicated that some of the most influential Soviet leaders were still in favor of drastic steps to solve Polish problems. General Jaruzelski was seen as not keeping up with promises he had made to the Soviets when martial law was imposed. The Polish regime did not apologize for this; instead it promptly demonstrated that the quotations used by *Novo vremyé* were taken out of context and that one of the quotations had never in fact appeared in *Polityka*.[7] This rebuttal to Moscow, explained Bernard Margueritte, "gave Mr. Rakowski and General Jaruzelski greater credibility in the Polish public's eyes. Many of those who condemned the government are prompted to ponder and to wonder whether the reform policy adopted by General Jaruzelski, however inadequate it may appear to them, is not in fact, in view of the Soviet attacks, the maximum that can realistically be done at present in the country."[8]

General Jaruzelski had never enjoyed Moscow's full trust and confidence. He was willing to follow the general line of Soviet foreign policy and to see that the communist system was securely entrenched in Poland, but as an experienced politician he sought to preserve a balance between Soviet support and popular consent for his leadership. He promised and delivered the destruction of Solidarity, yet explained his action as a "lesser evil"—leaving no doubts as to what greater evil he was trying to prevent. Russian atrocities committed against Poland constitute a substantial portion of Poland's history.

The post–World War II history of Eastern Europe provides plenty of evidence that genuine popularity for a communist regime offers much more stability and effectiveness than complete harmony with Moscow. Jaruzelski's policy, known as "Kádárization," called for great cooperation with the Soviet Union in exchange for a free hand in Poland. The general did not eliminate "counterrevolution"; this may have been deliberate, intended to show that his concept of communism was not identical to the Soviet ideal and that, after all, he was not a Soviet general in Polish uniform. His policies, both foreign and domestic, were full of contradictions—showing on one hand loyalty to Moscow and the principles of Soviet ideology and, on the other, political pragmatism. Pursuing practical goals, General Jaruzelski often irritated Moscow with his rhetorical insistence on national reconciliation and economic reforms. Unable to achieve quick approval for his policies from the majority of Polish society, he was notoriously handicapped in his dealings with Moscow. In Poland he projected the unpopular image of a Soviet agent; in Moscow he was distrusted as a Polish nationalist.

Cut off from Western economic help, General Jaruzelski reintegrated the country into the Soviet bloc; yet he gave a green light to the rapid expansion of private businesses. Poland's ideological conformity with the Soviet Union became faultless at the time when officially encouraged nationalism began to flourish. Most political prisoners were freed, and some new institutional arrangements, such as the constitutional tribunal, were established—all of which represented a substantial departure from the Soviet model. Three years after martial law was imposed, Polish-Soviet relations became more evenhanded, despite the strong preference of the new general secretary of the Soviet communist party, Konstantin Chernenko, for Brezhnevian ideological orthodoxy and strict compliance with the Soviet model and the Soviet foreign policy line.

Explaining Poland's close dependence on Soviet Russia was always the most difficult task of the Warsaw authorities. Hostility toward the Russians and toward communism is a basic fact of Polish life. The Russians were instrumental in partitioning Poland two hundred years ago; Russian troops suppressed all progressive social movements in the nineteenth century; and Soviet Russia invaded Poland in 1920 and in 1939 with Nazi Germany. Moscow is fully aware of the political mood in Poland; as a rule, the Soviets mistrust the Poles, even the Polish communists.

The pro-Soviet orientation of Polish foreign policy is presented by the regime as a matter of choice rather than necessity. The benefits of Poland's membership in the Soviet bloc, according to Poland's former foreign minister Stefan Olszowski, include,

> A new conception of Polish foreign policy . . . born out of the experience of the September [1939] calamity, the terror of the occupation, the threat of biological extermination, and out of thoughts on the course of events. It was formed by the socialist left wing, together with all the other democratic forces of the nation. Three fundamental thoughts lie at the roots of the programmatic reorientation of Poland's foreign policy. First: The above conception was a program for the return of Poland to historical Polish territory situated on the Odra and Nysa rivers and on the Baltic. The implementation and perpetuation of this program was one of the basic national tasks of foreign policy during the postwar period. Second: It was a program of permanently establishing friendly Polish-Soviet relations. This reorientation has been achieved. Third: It was a program whose implementation in accordance with the Yalta Conference declaration [1945] was meant to guarantee that Germany will never be able to disturb world peace.[9]

General Jaruzelski's weak and unpopular regime had no alternative to siding firmly with the Soviet Union. Poland's weakness provided new impetus for political and economic integration within the Warsaw Pact and the Council for Mutual Economic Assistance (CMEA), as well as with Moscow through bilateral agreements. Angry at Washington's punitive economic measures against Poland, Warsaw viciously criticized the United States, and President Reagan personally. The traditionally moderate tone of Poland's anti-U.S. propaganda was no longer followed by Polish officials, who without exception attacked the U.S. policy. Poland became an obedient tool in the hands of Soviet diplomacy, providing political, and probably economic, support for such Soviet clients as Afghanistan, Angola, and Nicaragua.

When Stefan Olszowski arrived in Kabul, Afghanistan, in June 1984, he expressed Poland's full support for Kabul's communist regime, describing Afghanistan and Poland as two victims of an "undeclared war"

waged by the United States.[10] At a dinner honoring Angolan president
José Eduardo dos Santos, General Jaruzelski accused the United States of
imperialism, intervention, and blackmail. "Using the slogan of anticommunist crusade," said Jaruzelski,

> American imperialism is striving to alter the balance of forces in the
> world and achieve military superiority, and it is creating new phases of
> the arms race. In its expansionist policy conducted from a position
> of strength, it is declaring various corners of the globe to be its spheres of
> "vital interest." It is illegally applying economic restrictions, conducting
> political boycotts, and carrying out propaganda aggression. It is not
> holding back from armed intervention and open interference in the do-
> mestic affairs of sovereign states.[11]

Similar anti-U.S. opinions were expressed in Warsaw to the visiting leader
of the Sandinista National Liberation Front, Daniel Ortega. Washington
was charged with rejecting peaceful solutions to the conflict in Central
America, in addition to the usual charges of imperialism, interference in
domestic affairs, and violation of other states' sovereignty.[12] In the realm
of foreign policy, Warsaw reduced itself to Moscow's transmission belt;
and even this was blamed on the United States. "There are very few people," stated General Jaruzelski, "who have done so much to convince socialist countries about the need for better integration. . . . If there were a
medal [for such services], the first one would go to President Reagan."[13]
Poland's political integration within the Soviet bloc required that it adopt
a confrontational posture toward the United States.

The glorification of the Soviet Union and its allegedly peaceful policy,
derived from its "philosophy of struggle for peace,"[14] is another by-product
of Chernenko's neo-Stalinist attempt to restore monolithic order within
the Soviet empire. The rituals of Soviet veneration were carried daily
by the Polish press, and frequently repeated by Polish officials. Following General Jaruzelski's visit to Moscow in May 1984, Polish commentary characterized the Polish-Soviet alliance as "natural . . . [and] rooted
in common ideology, common political interests, the brotherhood of
arms, . . . geography, complementary economic interests, and the common
dangers posed by U.S. imperialism and its allied nationalistic forces in the
FRG." In return, Konstantin Chernenko declared that the Soviet Union
was ready "to deal a most determined rebuff to all who dare lay hands on
the independence of . . . fraternal Poland."[15]

This "complete identity" of views on international issues did not include unequivocal Soviet approval of Jaruzelski's domestic policies. Moscow welcomed the stability and economic progress achieved by Jaruzelski,
but his frequent amnesties for political prisoners and his dialogue with the

Catholic church were never fully approved by the Soviet leadership. Jaruzelski's political inconsistencies fueled Soviet doubts about his commitment to communism and the Soviet Union. The Soviets never ceased to suspect Jaruzelski of nationalist sympathies; they believed his policies were motivated by geostrategic considerations in Eastern Europe. The Soviets' ambivalence toward Poland was expressed in a joint communiqué issued at the end of Jaruzelski's talks in Moscow. Though both parties had "identical" views on international issues, on Polish internal matters they achieved only "complete mutual understanding"—not agreement, which might have implied that the Soviets approved of Polish socialism.[16]

Nevertheless, while he was in Moscow General Jaruzelski signed a fifteen-year economic pact with the Soviets. This pact closely linked the Polish and Soviet economies for three consecutive Polish and Soviet five-year plans. Tightening the economic bonds with Moscow was presented in Poland as a way to strengthen economic security, because the Soviet economy, according to *Trybuna ludu,* "is free from crises and tremors."[17] It was implied that Poland's economic cooperation with the West in the 1970s was responsible for Poland's social and economic crises, and that close relations with Moscow and other Soviet-bloc partners would ensure Poland's well-being and political stability. In practice, Jaruzelski made Poland an economic ward of Moscow, forcing Polish enterprises to coordinate their production and investment policies with Soviet firms. Within six months after the agreement, 63 major Polish companies signed long-term contracts with the Soviets. The basic goal of the agreement—to strengthen Poland's dependence on the Soviet economy—was derived from the political goal to reorient the Polish economy geographically from West to East.

In 1985, trade with the Soviets accounted for 37 percent of the global foreign turnover. Poland's inability to trade with the West allowed the Soviet Union to recapture and dominate Polish markets and production. The structure of Poland's economic relations and the character of its industry were substantially altered. Cut off from Western technology, Poland's products became noncompetitive even within the Soviet bloc, allowing the Soviet Union to monopolize the supply of fuels and other essential raw materials to Poland. Soviet orders kept Poland's heavy industry alive. About three hundred Polish industrial plants, which turned out more than 30 percent of Poland's total industrial production, worked directly for the Soviets. At the same time, however, owing to the breakdown of Poland's economy in the early 1980s and the low technological level of Polish products, Poland's share in overall Soviet trade decreased from 10 percent in 1980 to 8 percent in 1985, falling behind East Germany, Czechoslovakia, and even Bulgaria.[18]

Adopted in May 1984, the "Long-term Program for the Development of Economic and Scientific-Technological Cooperation Between Poland and the Soviet Union until the Year 2000" revitalized the Polish-Soviet Intergovernmental Commission for Economic and Scientific-Technological Cooperation. This organization assumed direct responsibility for economic relations between the two countries. Emphasis was placed on the special role accorded to jointly managed and jointly financed enterprises. More than 220 projects were agreed upon by the end of 1985, making every major branch of Polish industry an appendix to its Soviet counterpart. For example, the Polish shipbuilding, steel, computer, heavy and transportation machinery construction, chemical, and petrochemical industries were directly linked with the Soviet Union. In effect, the Polish government lost control over most of its economy.

The Soviet emphasis on economic coordination appeared to be another element of the Brezhnev Doctrine, limiting the sovereignty of the East European satellites. Political and military ties between Moscow and its clients were supplemented with an excessive, one-sided economic dependence on the USSR. In particular, Poland's economic relations with the Soviet Union assumed the character of colonial dependency.

Another aspect of Poland's growing dependence on the Soviet Union was its involvement in the "New International Economic Order." This Soviet strategy, directed toward less developed countries, envisioned the development of economic relations providing Moscow with political leverage and access to raw materials in Latin America, Africa, and Asia. Presenting the global foreign debt issue as one of the world's most important economic problems and a testimony to Western exploitation, Moscow and its satellites proposed an open-door policy for other states to participate in economic coordination arranged by the CMEA countries. Poland concluded a number of cartel agreements with Third World countries, and increased its aid to Cuba substantially, perhaps by as much as 89 percent.[19]

During his April 1984 visit to Moscow, General Jaruzelski invited Soviet leader Chernenko to Warsaw, but the latter's poor health prior to his death in March 1985 precluded his trip. Consequently, Mikhail S. Gorbachev got a firsthand view of Poland's normalization. On 26 April 1985, Poland hosted leaders of the six other Warsaw Treaty Organization members, who renewed the pact for another twenty years. Besides Gorbachev, the Soviet delegation included Foreign Minister Andrei A. Gromyko and Konstantin V. Rusakov, secretary of the Soviet Central Committee in charge of relations with other ruling communist parties.

The Jaruzelski-Gorbachev meeting produced qualified Soviet support for Warsaw and its policies designed to overcome "the effects of the crisis, [and designed] for stability and for strengthening the position of socialism."[20] However, the Soviet boss was irritated by the continuing political tensions in Poland, and refused to give Jaruzelski his undivided support. In particular, the Poles had failed to restrain the Catholic church, revitalize the communist party, and modernize their armed forces, as Jaruzelski had promised Chernenko. After more than three years of martial law, the Warsaw regime appeared to be paralyzed by its inability to mobilize society, eliminate opposition, and cure the country's economic ills.

The joint Polish-Soviet communiqué made no specific reference to Poland's internal situation. General Jaruzelski failed to secure a strong and clear Soviet endorsement to use against hard-liners like Stefan Olszowski, who were therefore able to subvert his policies. On the contrary, Gromyko met with Olszowski to assess his political strength and aspirations, and to demonstrate that Moscow had a contact independent of Jaruzelski. The long-expected political purge of Poland's hard-liners had to be suspended. Jaruzelski was told to produce more tangible results before the new Soviet leader would extend his undivided support. The Polish leader was given extra time to curb the influence of the church, restore the leading role of the party, scale down the military nature of his regime, and improve the economic situation.

Still, Gorbachev's visit marked a significant improvement in Polish-Soviet relations. As one observer pointed out, "The Poland of General Jaruzelski has certainly come a long way in the eyes of Moscow, since it was harshly admonished by the Soviet leadership in March 1981 and again in June 1981 [in a letter signed by Leonid Brezhnev and sent to all Polish Central Committee members], when the Polish regime was called on to 'reverse the course of events' in the country."[21]

Gorbachev's evenhanded approach to Poland's main political factions only postponed the purge. A skillful tactician, General Jaruzelski presented the Soviet visits as an endorsement of his leadership. Six months later, he outmaneuvered Olszowski, who was relieved of his seat on the Politburo and his post as foreign minister. Two months after this, in January 1986, Jaruzelski appointed Włodzimierz Natorf as Poland's ambassador to the Soviet Union, replacing another notorious Stalinist, Stanisław Kociolek. The latter's departure from this important diplomatic post ended a political career that included direct responsibility for killing Polish workers during the 1970 strikes and outspoken criticism of Solidarity. As Poland's ambassador to Moscow, Kociolek was known for his attempts to subvert Jaruzelski and his moderate political course.

This partial purge of hard-liners provided Jaruzelski with useful political flexibility just a few months before the tenth congress of the Polish communist party, and demonstrated to Gorbachev that the Polish leader knew how to survive without Soviet help. His new power was one of the reasons why he was welcomed in Moscow in March 1986 at the 27th congress of the Soviet communist party like a partner rather than a suspect, and was permitted to address the congress as the first foreign speaker. This honor symbolically restored Poland's position as the principal ally of Moscow. It was a clear sign that the Soviets had accepted Polish nationalism and the irreconcilable differences between the Soviet and Polish socialist models. In a sense, Jaruzelski finally was able to deal with the Soviets from a position of strength.

The tenth party congress in Poland in early July 1986 was the culmination of General Jaruzelski's five-year effort to rebuild the party, and the coronation of his *Ostpolitik*. Unlike the previous party congress in July 1981, it was a well-orchestrated event, with no democratic pretenses and no surprises.

Jaruzelski consolidated his power and the party, as he had promised the Soviets, by appointing three more generals to the ruling Politburo, placing them in charge of internal affairs, defense, and ideology. Aside from the military, all Politburo members owed their political careers to Jaruzelski, and their selection indicated their full support of his policies. The delegates were instructed to change the party statute that limited tenure in all party offices to two terms. Under the old rule, General Jaruzelski would have to retire as first secretary in 1991; under the new law he could stay in office until 1996.

Mikhail Gorbachev was the key foreign guest at the Polish congress. His endorsement of General Jaruzelski's leadership was without reservation. He personally addressed his congratulations to the Polish leader and publicly embraced Jaruzelski as a friend. However, Gorbachev made it clear that Moscow's tolerance for Polish socialism would not extend so far as to include a revival of Solidarity or any other tampering with the basic canons of the Soviet system in Poland. Invoking the Brezhnev Doctrine of limited sovereignty, Gorbachev told the Poles that socialism is both an internal order and "an international reality" that "manifests itself as an alliance of countries closely linked by political, economic, cultural, and defense interests." He also said that "to threaten the socialist system, to try to undermine it from outside and wrench a country away from the socialist community means to encroach not only on the will of the people, but also on the entire postwar arrangement and, in the last analysis, on peace."[22]

The issue of Poland's sovereignty was brought to Gorbachev's attention by an open letter written by Stefan Bartkowski, a well-known Polish intellectual, former chairman of the Polish journalists' union, and a member of the dissident group Experience and Future. On behalf of two hundred Polish writers, Bartkowski asked the Soviet leader for "the complete implementation of the Yalta accords, which implies the recognition of [Poland's] status as an independent state whose powers are decided on by elections proper to parliamentary democracies." Independent Poland would "expect from the Soviet Union infinitely smaller concessions than those the Soviet Union granted Finland," and the Poles would not leave the Warsaw Pact or try to alter existing borders in Europe. The alternative, namely the continuing Sovietization of Poland, would lead to a Polish-Soviet confrontation that would threaten the vital security interests of the Soviet state. The report concluded by stating that "the Poles have not given up their aspirations of freedom," but that they "are not interested in confrontation and want to be a friendly neighbor of the Soviet Union."[23]

In 1985, the Soviets were still unable to accept the simple truth that their system and ideology had not worked in Poland. The forceful imposition of totalitarian socialism was counterproductive to Soviet security and added to the economic burden of the empire. Moreover, Marxism-Leninism had become the world's most uninspiring ideological system. It was demoralizing, rather than mobilizing, societies, and its deadly effects on economic progress and political consensus were leading to apathy and inertia. The Soviet leaders' great arrogance and pathological insecurity closely resembled the narrow-mindedness of the last tsars, who eventually provoked a revolution.

Jaruzelski's show-of-force maneuverings and manipulations consolidated his power and resurrected the communist facade and the appearance of friendly relations with the Soviets. Meanwhile Polish society developed alternatives to official patterns of interaction and subterranean economic activities, which for many became their primary source of income; it also developed widespread anti-Soviet feelings. The country became a hotbed of anticommunist barriers to the Soviet Union's security and international credibility.

Growing anti-Russian feelings in Poland were countered by several waves of pro-Soviet propaganda. The alliance between Poland and the USSR had been glorified as the cornerstone of Poland's independence, territorial integrity, and international status. In exchange for this propaganda, Moscow was willing to restore for General Jaruzelski and his country the status of the first ally of Moscow. During the 27th congress of the CPSU, the Polish delegation was treated with special honors to demonstrate Soviet approval of Warsaw's domestic policies.[24]

One minor concession to Polish nationalism was approved by Moscow. When returning from the CPSU congress, General Jaruzelski visited the Lithuanian city of Vilnius.[25] Until 1939, Vilnius was a Polish city, the birthplace of many distinguished Poles. It was a symbol of the Polish-Lithuanian commonwealth, which, until the partitions at the end of the eighteenth century, checked Russian territorial expansion toward the west.

Once Poland's status in Moscow was firmly secured, Warsaw moved to reduce anti-U.S. propaganda and to initiate a major foreign policy campaign. Acting as a spokesman for the entire Warsaw Pact, General Jaruzelski offered to trade a reduction in the number of its tanks for a reduction in NATO's airplanes. He said, "We know the West believes that there is a preponderance of the Warsaw Pact in tanks. We believe that the NATO countries have a preponderance in certain kinds of aircraft, especially bombers. The first step could be taken with those two categories."[26]

The Jaruzelski plan was seen by the Soviet bloc countries as complementary to the mutual balanced force reduction (MBFR) talks, which focused on cutting the numbers of troops rather than weapons. The plan symbolized Poland's return to the status of the second most important member of the Warsaw Pact, with special responsibility for negotiating the reduction of conventional weapons in Europe. It was also evidence that full harmony and mutual trust between Warsaw and Moscow had been achieved. As at the end of 1950s, Poland was allowed to act more independently in foreign and domestic affairs.

The symptoms of fundamental changes in Polish-Soviet relations went beyond the new foreign policy initiatives pronounced by Warsaw. After more than four decades of falsifications, in 1987 the Polish and Soviet authorities reached agreement on filling in the blank spots in the two countries' history. Some of the most painful issues relating to the Soviet treatment of the Poles suddenly received attention in the official press. Among the blank spots addressed by the authorities was the disbandment of the Polish communist party and the execution of about fifteen thousand Polish communists in 1938; the 1939 Nazi-Soviet pact; the Katyn massacre of fifteen thousand Polish officers; the deportation of 1.6 million Poles in the areas occupied by the Red Army during 1939–41; Polish-Soviet relations during World War II; and the consequences of Stalinism. For the first time in history, Soviet crimes against the Polish nation were publicly admitted, permanently changing the official image of Soviet Russia and the perception of friendship between the two countries.

The Soviets, however, continued to reject any idea of compromise between the government and the opposition. The newly granted freedom to act in the international arena had no effect on domestic affairs, which were dominated by a deep socioeconomic cleavage and a prevailing distrust of the communist authorities. Minor concessions in Poland's foreign policy could not offset the deep internal deadlock that threatened the stability and economic well-being of the country. The Jaruzelski regime experimented with a variety of alternatives to the relegalization of the outlawed Solidarity, but it eventually became apparent that the only solution was a return to the *status quo ante bellum.*

Soviet leader Mikhail Gorbachev's six-day visit to Poland in July 1988 was a historic event, indicating that Moscow had finally come to the conclusion that Poland would not be governable without Solidarity and free elections. During his stay in Poland the Soviet leader approved union pluralism and significantly modified the Brezhnev Doctrine. "Today," stated Gorbachev, "equal rights, independence, and the joint solving of the problems before us are an undeniable rule of our relations. They are becoming free of paternalism and are fully geared to voluntary partnership based on interests."[27] The period of one-sided friendship in Polish-Soviet relations was over, and both countries were moving into the realm of realpolitik.

This new chapter in bilateral relations was agreed upon during the brief working visit to Moscow at the end of April 1989 by General Jaruzelski and several other top officials representing the communist authorities.[28] The new atmosphere was confirmed in July 1989, when the Polish dissident Adam Michnik, "someone who has been called a revisionist, ideological saboteur, agent provocateur, and imperialist spy . . . for at least two decades,"[29] visited Moscow to attend a conference on East-West security issues.

The international significance of these developments was primarily in the new definition of bilateral relations, which no longer resembled colonial patterns. The new model of coexistence was based on common interests in fostering stability in Europe and on mutual compromise and understanding between Poles and Russians. For this reason, the Solidarity-led government that took power in August 1989 pledged to respect the international obligations assumed by its predecessor. In November 1989, Poland's new prime minister, Tadeusz Mazowiecki, the former head of Solidarity's "shadow cabinet," visited Moscow. During the visit he emphasized the "prime importance" to Poland of good relations with the Soviet Union, but stressed that it was necessary to clear up several "painful issues," including Katyn and the 1939 Nazi-Soviet pact, which Poland wished to be declared null and void from its inception.[30]

The new government in Warsaw accepted the fact that Moscow had certain strong strategic and economic interests in Poland; however, this should not prevent the two countries from arranging their mutual relations in an egalitarian fashion that respects the sovereignty of both nations. The noncommunist government in Poland hoped to fashion future Polish-Soviet relations on the Finnish model of coexistence between a smaller state and a superpower. Poland would like to be a useful, nonthreatening neighbor respected for its commitment to independence and reduction in tension between East and West.

PART II

Solidarity and the United States

CHAPTER THREE

United States Support for Solidarity

United States policy toward Poland during the critical months of the 1980–81 crisis was shaped by several international developments, but above all by the decline of East-West relations following the Soviet invasion of Afghanistan. United States grain shipments to the Soviet Union were embargoed and exports of high technology were curbed, thus ending a decade of détente between the superpowers. The Polish government immediately found itself in a precarious position, trying to appear loyal to the Soviets while remaining on good terms with the United States. Good relations with Washington had always been Warsaw's main source of prestige and hard currency. Continuing access to Western markets and credits had sustained the Polish economy and its communist rulers during the 1970s, when Poland increased its net hard-currency debt from $760 million in 1971 to over $20 billion nine years later.[1]

The 1980 workers' revolt came after this prolonged economic crisis, and demonstrated how fragile and insecure the communist regimes in Eastern Europe and the Soviet Union really were. Poland was a particularly good example of the inherent vulnerability of the communist system. The workers' uprising against the state—which claimed to be an embodiment of their interests—was without doubt the most embarrassing development in the Soviet empire since World War II. Of course, the communist regime in Poland had another role besides pretending to represent the working class. Its main mission was to guarantee Soviet geostrategic interests in Eastern Europe. The Soviet resolution to preserve imperial order in Eastern Europe by any means was the chief barrier to change and to peaceful Western involvement in Poland and other countries. Several East European attempts to reduce Soviet control resulted in military invasions, reducing the U.S. role to impotent handwringing.

United States policy toward Poland was complicated by the 1980 U.S. presidential campaign. Both candidates used the Polish crisis for political capital, making demonstrative gestures and statements, and calling for unrealistic retaliatory steps in the event that the revolt was crushed—unrealistic because they knew that Moscow's hegemony in Poland could not be challenged. A Soviet invasion of Poland would be another reflection of U.S. weakness.

The official U.S. policy toward Poland, however, was an example of prudent diplomacy. It recognized geopolitical limits but took full advantage of new opportunities created by the internal developments in Poland. In principle, the United States followed a low-key policy; it used economic levers to restrain the Polish government from suppressing Solidarity, and it warned Moscow against a military invasion of Poland. The United States adopted a policy of differentiation between the Soviet Union and Poland. On the one hand, it stressed that Moscow's violation of human rights and of the sovereignty of smaller nations like Afghanistan would not be subsidized by U.S. credits, grain, and technology; on the other hand, the Polish regime's concessions to the striking workers and its general adherence to the August 1980 agreement with Solidarity were rewarded with generous U.S. economic aid.

In September 1980 President Carter announced that the United States would increase its foreign credits to Poland from $550 million in fiscal year 1979–80 to $670 million in 1980–81. (The Polish government had requested $3 billion in low-interest loans for the next three years.) The U.S. aid covered four areas: new credits for grain purchases; a rescheduling of Poland's foreign debt; an emergency food program; and a doubling of Poland's fishing quotas in Alaskan waters. This package was defined by the Polish-American Congress as "a reflection of the [U.S.] moral commitment that is a necessary part of any effective human rights program."[2] An additional loan of $325 million was organized for Poland by a consortium of Western banks. However, 85 cents of every dollar borrowed by the Poles went to servicing their foreign debt.

The United States was cautiously taking major responsibility for assisting the Polish government in handling its economic crisis in hopes that the combined impact of Solidarity and Western economic aid would substantially reduce Poland's dependence on the Soviet Union. The Carter administration followed a policy, popular in the 1970s, known as the Sonnenfeldt Doctrine, which advocated subsidies to the communist regimes in Eastern Europe as a means of stabilizing this region and, in the long run, encouraging its emancipation from Soviet hegemony. The revolt of the Polish workers and the official recognition of the free and independent trade union appeared to be fruits of the decade of détente and political benefits of the hard-currency credits extended to Warsaw. Additional loans were seen in the West as a way to secure the political gains of Solidarity and support the Western policy toward Poland.

Since 1970 Poland had enjoyed tariff concessions, export privileges, generous fishing quotas in U.S. waters, and numerous cultural and scientific agreements with the United States and the countries of Western Europe. Poland seemed to be slowly becoming an economic satellite of the West while remaining Moscow's political client. Solidarity's successful challenge to the leading role of the communist party promised major alterations of European bloc politics. Consequently, Western policy during 1980–81 was designed to keep Solidarity alive by giving financial support to a regime willing to cooperate with the union and willing to deter Soviet aggression.

A fundamental reform of the communist system appeared inevitable. The formation of an independent union in Poland was unprecedented in any communist-ruled state and a milestone toward democracy. Supported by over ten million Polish workers (about 60 percent of the entire labor force), the union appeared to be a formidable political force leading Poland away from the party's monopoly of all political and economic power—and thus away from Moscow.

Poland's political strains came on the heels of the serious economic difficulties that affected the entire Eastern bloc, including the Soviet Union. The problems haunting the communist leaders were considered so serious that permanent compromise with Solidarity was regarded as the only viable option. Washington was ready to pay the communists for allowing Polish workers to soften the Soviet system, and hoped to use the Polish crisis to foster democratization in Eastern Europe. Democratic sentiments in that region, and in Poland particularly, are very strong among all social classes, including the working class, which had firsthand experience of the selfishness and incompetence of the party.

The United States, in effect, sided with the Polish government, as long as the authorities in Warsaw faithfully followed the letter and spirit of the August 1980 agreement with the workers—and as long as Soviet tanks did not roll into Poland. United States credits and other forms of economic assistance were the only avenue of influence available to Washington. During the Carter administration, economic aid was simply viewed as an instrument for stimulating political changes in Poland; the U.S.

government did not appear to be concerned about the purely economic aspects of Polish-U.S. relations, or about Poland's creditworthiness.

The Western banks, however, did not share the official fascination with the political transition taking place in Poland. Their attention was focused on the financial side of Poland's labor unrest. The country was still considered to be in a viable economic condition because of its strong industrial base, which so far was little affected by the strikes and the emergence of Solidarity. Still, the Western banking community began to express its uneasiness about the growing instability, which could undermine the economic fabric of the country. Because their primary concern was to have their money back, the bankers looked favorably on the alternative of a Soviet invasion. Moscow, it was concluded, would never allow Poland to default on its Western debt, since radical steps by a Soviet satellite would undermine the extensive, lucrative financial relations Moscow had with the West. Ironically, Western big business sided with the communists.

The U.S. working class, however, sided with Solidarity against the Polish government and Moscow, and consequently against the Carter administration. Longshoremen, for example, boycotted all ships carrying cargo to and from Poland, including shipments of U.S. grain sold on credit by the government to the Polish authorities. Moreover, the U.S. longshoremen appealed to international labor leaders to follow their example.

Support for Solidarity was organized by the AFL-CIO, which by the end of 1980 had contributed $150,000 to the Polish workers, plus numerous gifts such as printing presses and communication equipment. Individual member unions of the AFL-CIO made their own collections for various forms of assistance. For example, the Ladies Garment Workers Union collected $10,000 and the United Auto Workers $25,000; these funds were funneled directly to the Polish workers. The official position of the U.S. government was that "these several thousand dollars could do a great deal of harm."[3]

The Soviets concluded that some kind of international conspiracy was underwriting internal developments in Poland. Lane Kirkland, president of the AFL-CIO, had expressed opposition to "quiet diplomacy" and encouraged strong public support for the independent union in Poland. Tom Kahn, assistant to the president of the AFL-CIO, had stated: "The notion that the Soviet Union would invade Poland because the AFL-CIO gave a printing press to the Polish workers shows the analytical level to which the State Department had fallen... Did anyone think that, having received an appeal from the Polish workers, we would turn our backs on them and say 'no'? That would amount to telling the Polish workers they should submit to tyranny."[4] It was the position and actions of the U.S.

working class, not those of the politically cautious administration or conservative business, that triggered Soviet and Polish accusations of external interference in Poland's domestic affairs.

Articles written by the infamous Petrov attacked "anti-socialist elements in Poland [that] seek to coordinate their actions with reactionary Polish emigration and with subversive centers functioning in the West." The alleged purpose of Western support for Solidarity was "to inflict damage on the socialist gains of the Polish people, to try to push Poland off the road it took, by the will of the people, after its liberation from the German-Fascist invaders."[5] The Polish response was more balanced, pointing out differences between the official U.S. policy and the actions of the U.S. unions. A Polish official summarized the situation by expressing gratitude for the U.S. government's "noninterference." "This attitude was correct. I wouldn't hesitate to say useful, even responsible. The approach was right—that this was a problem to be settled between Poles and by Poles." The AFL-CIO, however, was charged with interfering in Poland's internal affairs and identified by the Polish authorities as an "antisocialist force" exploiting Poland's unrest to undermine the socialist order.[6]

The positions taken toward Poland by the Carter administration, the banking community, and the American unions reflect the profound political dilemma faced by the West. On one hand, there was a high degree of sympathy and support for the Polish nation and its relentless opposition to Soviet domination and communist oppression. On the other hand, the West lacked a comprehensive, long-term strategy for dealing with Poland and the other Eastern European nations in the Soviet bloc. The West's good intentions could not be transformed into a coordinated effort to help emancipate Poland from communist control. Consequently, right from the beginning of the Polish crisis, the United States' contradictory efforts reduced the West's ability to influence events in Poland. Once again, the West was unprepared for another indigenous challenge to the imperial Soviet system in Eastern Europe.

Despite the United States' restrained response to the Polish crisis, the authorities in Warsaw, alarmed by the internal developments, began to revert to cold-war foreign policy patterns. Weak and insecure, the regime could no longer practice détente as East-West tensions mounted. After Ronald Reagan's victory in the 1980 U.S. presidential election, the United States became a convenient scapegoat for Poland's troubles. Deteriorating U.S.-Soviet relations forced Warsaw to abandon its hopes for partial independence from Moscow's anti-U.S. policy, and the first indications of a belligerently anti-U.S. attitude surfaced in Warsaw at the end of 1980. The Polish press continued to argue that there was no realistic alternative to dealing with Solidarity, and in principle adopted a wait-and-see position with respect to Soviet-U.S. relations; however, new anti-U.S. rhetoric accused President-elect Reagan of seeking world supremacy for the United States.

Warsaw wanted to see East-West tensions lessened, for fear of a freeze on Western credits and growing Soviet demands for unequivocal support for its foreign policy. With the return of international tension, Moscow began to view Poland as a destabilizing factor in East-West relations. Above all, the Soviets could not tolerate a bilateral Polish-U.S. dialogue at a time when U.S.-Soviet relations were overtly antagonistic. Rupturing Polish-U.S. relations could allow Moscow to exert greater influence on Warsaw; the best means to that end was to have Polish authorities accuse the United States of interfering in Poland's internal affairs. The Soviet aim was to characterize Solidarity as a counterrevolutionary force, directed by Washington—a threat not only to Poland but to the national security of the Soviet Union. A Soviet military invasion of Poland could then claim to be defensive.

The objectives established by the Carter administration with respect to Poland remained unchanged when the Republicans took over in January 1981. The United States continued to monitor the Polish situation closely, attempting only to prevent a military solution of the crisis and to relieve the Poles' economic hardships. This bipartisan policy was officially supported by the U.S. Senate, which on 27 March 1982 issued a resolution endorsing the Reagan administration's offer of humanitarian assistance, provided there was no internal repression or foreign intervention. The resolution also expressed confidence that the Polish problem would be solved by the Polish people alone, and that the use of force against Solidarity would be viewed as a violation of both the United Nations charter and the Helsinki Accord.

There was speculation, however, both in the West and in Poland that the Reagan administration was actually playing a double game: giving out official warnings against a possible Soviet invasion, while in reality welcoming another Afghanistan-like Soviet military action against a disobedient client state. It was argued that a Soviet move against Poland would add credibility to Reagan's more assertive policy aims vis-à-vis the Soviets and facilitate congressional approval of greater military expenditures.[7]

When confronted with this allegation, U.S. officials insisted that, in the words of Secretary of State Alexander Haig, "Any application of force in the internal affairs of the Polish people could have unforeseen and most dangerous consequences, and I don't know of any responsible official in this Administration that would welcome that outcome." Haig said that the United States would do nothing to "alleviate the suffering and the anguish of the Polish people at this difficult time."[8] This position was reiterated in the official statement issued by the White House on the Polish situation: "We would like to make clear to all concerned our view that external intervention in Poland, or any measures aimed at suppressing the Polish people, would necessarily cause deep concern to all those interested in the peaceful development of Poland, and could have a grave effect on the whole course of East-West relations."[9]

This policy soon became evident when Poland's vice-premier, Mieczysław Jagielski, arrived in Washington in early April 1981 to ask for more economic help. The Reagan administration immediately agreed to provide, in addition to the $670 million in credits for purchasing food approved by the Carter administration, $70 million in surplus butter and dried milk, and to reschedule about $80 million in debt payments due by 30 June 1981.[10] Summarizing his visit to Washington, Vice-premier Jagielski said: "We expect assistance from our friend, the United States."[11] The total volume of U.S.-Polish economic transactions in 1981 exceeded $1.3 billion.

The United States had consistently tried to reduce the internal tensions and economic hardships in Poland so as to decrease internal polarization and the possibility of a Soviet invasion. At the same time, the Reagan administration made it clear that suppression of Solidarity, whether by Polish or Soviet forces, would automatically result in the suspension of Western aid. This policy was endorsed by all the other NATO countries. In addition, the members of NATO decided to link the prospects for East-West arms-reduction talks to the manner in which the Eastern bloc resolved the Polish crisis.

Further, the United States did not hesitate to express concern about the Soviets' threats against Poland. A good example was the U.S. State Department's response to the 5 June 1981 letter from the Central Committee of the Soviet communist party to the Central Committee of the Polish United Workers' Party, in which the Soviets directly threatened a military invasion unless the Poles could "mobilize all the healthy forces in society to resist the class enemy and combat counterrevolution."[12] The State Department characterized the Soviet letter as "threatening" and as constituting "interference in the internal affairs of Poland . . . Such interference is inconsistent with the requirements of the Final Helsinki Act and accepted international behavior with regard to relations among sovereign states."[13]

The United States made it known that it saw no justification for any outside interference in Poland, and that it would not under any circumstances recognize the self-appointed Soviet right to determine the domestic system of the countries of the so-called socialist community, including Poland. In other words, the United States again rejected the Brezhnev Doctrine, which denies self-determination by Eastern European nations.

The Reagan administration had frequently expressed concerns about Warsaw Pact maneuvers conducted inside or around Poland to intimidate Solidarity as well as the Polish leadership. Several times during 1981, Soviet military forces appeared to be ready to invade. The U.S. policy was to publicize the level of Soviet military preparations for intervention without, however, appearing excessively alarmed—the mistake committed by the Carter administration in December 1980. Colonel Kuklinski had provided the Reagan administration with a great deal of insight into the Soviet leadership's political and military intentions.

The Polish government, however, had an inverted view of reality. Despite the fact that its military machine was poised to attack Poland, the Soviet Union was lauded as a partner and friend in a time of need. The United States became the primary target for hollow accusations of interference in Poland's internal affairs, including alleged support for a civil war that would have killed hundreds of thousands and starved millions. In the second half of 1981, the official Polish press followed the Soviet lead and began to make regular attacks on the Reagan administration. It claimed that the United States was behind Solidarity's destabilizing counterrevolution in Poland as well as on the entire European continent. The workers' uprising in Poland was in the official Polish view nothing more than a CIA-inspired plot to alter the balance of forces in Europe, restore capitalism, and frustrate arms-reduction talks with the Soviet Union. The Polish regime adjusted its foreign policy to remove any doubts about Warsaw's loyalty to Moscow. General Jaruzelski intended to convince his superiors in the Kremlin that his government and the Soviet leadership saw the situation in the same light. He assured Moscow that he was capable of resolving Poland's unrest without assistance from any other Warsaw Pact state.

The anti-U.S. hysteria sponsored by the Warsaw regime served as an ideological credential for handling the Polish workers' revolt. Still, the Poles hoped that the United States would recognize these accusations as no more than a ceremonial pronouncement demanded by Poland's relations with the Soviet Union. The Poles believed that official statements by a vassal regime are not to be taken seriously, so the Polish government saw nothing inconsistent in simultaneously making such pronouncements and requesting emergency food aid from Washington. In July 1981 the Reagan administration approved a shipment of 400,000 metric tons of corn worth $80 million, to be paid for in Polish currency. This transaction was considered to have "minimal" political implications and was held not to constitute U.S. involvement in the Polish crisis.[14]

The United States was careful not to enmesh itself too deeply in Polish affairs; the situation became progressively unpredictable as speculation about the impending Soviet intervention dominated the news. (Colonel Kuklinski provided Washington with an approximate date for the scheduled imposition of martial law.) The Reagan administration hoped to discourage Moscow from invading Poland, and cautiously avoided any provocation that the Soviets could use to justify an invasion. The main goal of U.S. policy toward Poland was to refrain from any word or action that would complicate the already delicate situation. The U.S. options were limited to public warnings about a possible Soviet attack and about the Warsaw Pact military buildup around Poland. After several such warnings were issued by the Carter and Reagan administrations, however, U.S. credibility began to decline; Washington appeared to be "crying wolf" too often.

Direct Soviet political and military pressure on Poland significantly altered the character of the Polish crisis. What began as a domestic Polish affair involving Polish workers and the regime in Warsaw rapidly escalated into an international crisis and a key East-West issue. The mobilization of Warsaw Pact forces had a direct impact on the balance of power in Europe, causing alarm within NATO. In addition, the West feared the consequences of war in Central Europe, especially protracted partisan warfare between the Polish nation and the Soviets, as well as the social and economic impact of a Soviet-occupied Poland. Secretary of State Alexander M. Haig cautioned the Soviet ambassador to the United States, Anatolii F. Dobrynin, that a Soviet invasion would mean "a return to the cold war situation at the very least."[15] The West European allies of the United States were even more apprehensive owing to the geographic proximity of the anticipated conflict, which could result in a brutal Soviet suppression of the Poles. A massive exodus of Poles to the West was expected to follow the Soviet invasion.

The irony of this internationalization of the Polish crisis was that the Polish government and even Solidarity had lost their initial importance. The United States ceased to subsidize a regime that seemed destined either to failure or to the commission of major crimes on behalf of its Soviet masters. As with the immediate post–World War II period, the Polish question was not in the hands of the Poles, but was rather a subject of bilateral U.S.-Soviet relations. Moscow accused the Reagan administration of trying to alter the geopolitical balance of power by wresting Poland from the communist system. This ominous charge implied that Moscow was prepared to use all means to reassert its hegemony in Poland. The

Soviets proclaimed the Solidarity union to be a counterrevolutionary organization manipulated by the CIA, and charged it with preparing to overthrow the socialist system in Poland, including the physical elimination of tens of thousands of communists and their supporters. The Soviet newspaper *Pravda* went so far as to state that the Polish events were of strategic importance for the United States and that President Reagan had organized a special working group headed by Vice-president George Bush to direct counterrevolution in Poland.[16]

The Soviet leadership assumed that the United States was responsible in great measure for the Polish situation. They therefore considered that any Soviet action against Poland would be defensive in character and aimed not at the Polish nation or the union, but only at the United States' supposed interference in Poland's internal affairs. Moreover, according to Moscow, the United States used the Polish situation to divert attention away from the Soviet peace proposals and other steps intended to ease international tensions and strengthen security in Europe.

These heavy-handed accusations that the United States was subverting the balance of power in Europe intimidated Washington's West European allies. The issue was not whether the Soviet analysis of the Polish situation was right or wrong; Moscow intended to project toughness and determination and to end the free labor movement in Poland regardless of international consequences. The Soviet message implied that the geographically remote United States was jeopardizing the security of the European members of NATO by giving even moral support to Solidarity. In effect, the Soviets confronted Western Europe with a question: Is your support for Solidarity worth jeopardizing your nations' security? Knowing the answer, Moscow acquired de facto Western European allies against Poland.

The European leaders preferred a return to the status quo in Poland, for fear of instability on the entire continent. This attitude prevailed in Europe during the entire nineteenth century, when Polish uprisings against the occupying powers were viewed with sympathy, but also with reservation. The West European capitals once more perceived Polish events as destabilizing and hopeless, and they were willing to witness the termination of the free union experiment since it seemed inconsistent with the prevailing international order. This attitude left the United States alone vis-à-vis Moscow, and significantly reduced Washington's ability to influence the outcome of the power struggle in Poland. The West Europeans' restraint also gave some credibility to the Soviet accusation of American meddling in Poland's domestic affairs.

The primary objective of U.S. policy toward Moscow regarding developments in Poland was to deter Soviet aggression. The United States put diplomatic pressure on Moscow and maintained a benevolent attitude toward the official regime in Warsaw. On numerous occasions the U.S. government warned the Soviets about the political and economic consequences of an attack on Poland. The makers of U.S. foreign policy apparently believed that a Soviet military invasion would restore the communist status quo, and thus endanger Western security.

Soviet behavior during the Polish crisis remarkably resembled the pattern that led up to the invasion of Czechoslovakia in 1968. When the Soviet leaders declared in June 1981 that Poland's leadership could no longer handle the crisis, Moscow was in effect invoking the Brezhnev Doctrine and assuming responsibility for Poland's fate. Moscow campaigned vigorously to halt the extraordinary congress of the Polish communist party, which was expected to espouse internal divisions within Poland's ruling elite and sanction the liberalization that had swept the country since August 1980. The 1968 invasion of Czechoslovakia was timed to prevent a similar "revisionist" congress and was intended to check the disintegration of Prague's monopolistic and pro-Soviet regime. In June 1981 Poland's internal situation entered a political state that from the Soviet perspective seemed to call for possible military action.

Lacking direct means of influence in Poland, the United States encouraged—with generous economic assistance—internal dialogue between the regime and Solidarity. Washington's purpose was to discourage the Polish regime's provocation of Solidarity, which seemed calculated to produce political radicalization of the union to the point that its political demands would give the regime a casus belli for internal or external intervention. The United States was seeking a peaceful resolution of the Polish crisis, encouraging a transition to political pluralism while warning Moscow against a repetition of the military solutions of the earlier crises in Hungary and Czechoslovakia. It was made clear that if physical force was used against the Polish nation, the Soviet Union would face its own economic problems—and those of Poland—alone, as well as the unspecified "grave effect on the whole course of East-West relations" quoted earlier.[17]

To demonstrate its goodwill and determination, the United States entered into several lucrative (for Poland) economic agreements with Warsaw in the second half of 1981. At the end of July 1981, the U.S. Senate adopted a resolution in favor of granting Poland emergency food assistance. One month later the United States agreed to postpone, for five to eight years, 90 percent of Poland's financial obligations due that year. The U.S.-Polish scientific cooperation begun in 1974 was extended at the seventh meeting of the mutual scientific-technological commission that ended on 2 October, and on 11 December the Polish and American academies of science concluded a five-year agreement on scientific exchange. The United States and Poland also signed an agreement regulating air transportation between the two countries. At the 7–8 December meeting of the Polish-American Trade Commission, Secretary of Commerce Malcolm Baldrige indicated that the United States would continue to suspend Polish debt payments, support Poland's application for membership in the International Monetary Fund, and extend $740 million in new credits to Poland for purchasing food and other agricultural products. The total volume of U.S.-Polish trade in 1981 exceeded $1.3 billion and was expected to grow, provided the internal conflict in Poland could be resolved peacefully.

On 13 December 1981, however, General Jaruzelski's regime declared martial law in Poland, terminating a sixteen-month experiment with democracy and free trade unions. In justifying this action, General Jaruzelski made no reference to the Soviet pressures on Poland or to alleged counterrevolutionary activities by the United States. Claiming that Polish governmental structures were disintegrating and that the economy was on the edge of collapse, he invoked his constitutional responsibility to declare martial law throughout Poland. Jaruzelski's statement, delivered on television, made no specific reference to Solidarity. Stressing the restoration of social order and economic well-being, the statement was designed to divert attention from the mass arrests and detention of the union's leadership. It emphasized continued reforms and "socialist renewal" under the condition of social discipline. Foreign governments were informed that martial law would remove internal threats to international peace and European cooperation.

Although the country was invaded and reconquered pursuant to direct orders from Moscow, the United States was subsequently blamed for instigating a bloody coup in Poland. For example, Valentin Zorin, a political observer on Soviet television, claimed that by using Solidarity as its proxy the United States intended to overthrow the existing social system and frustrate the fulfillment of Poland's obligations as a member of the Warsaw Pact, thus directly affecting the security and interests of all the Pact's member states. Zorin stated:

> The Polish authorities have documents at their disposal which in the near future may be studied by all unbiased people to see that the documents contain not only concrete and detailed plans for taking over power by people elected by no one and operating against the Polish Constitution,

but also lists of persons to be executed. These lists cover not tens or hundreds of people but a total of 80,000. Punitive operations had already been prepared practically which had they not been foiled would have led to a bloodbath in Poland.[18]

According to *Żołnierz wolności*, the Polish Army daily, "The imposition of martial law largely paralyzed the activities of U.S. special services on Polish territory."[19]

The Polish authorities considered that the United States approached the Polish issue as a factor in the strategic competition with the Soviet Union, directly bearing on the United States' internal allocation of its resources. The Reagan administration, according to Warsaw, needed to create "an atmosphere justifying high military expenditures while there are growing demands to reduce the state budget and to arrest inflation." The crisis in Poland had become a convenient tool for achieving a global advantage over the Soviet Union and for justifying increased military expenditures. Solidarity, the Polish regime asserted, became an instrument of U.S. foreign policy, the purpose of which was to reaffirm Washington's global supremacy by "rolling back communism" in Poland.[20]

Martial law was the final step in the long strategy of wearing out and encouraging political radicalism among the national leaders of the union. The regime welcomed and contributed to Poland's economic difficulties, accusing Solidarity of resisting reforms and mutual agreements. When presented with the dilemma of either backtracking or taking a more assertive approach to the authorities (depending on popular support), the union was compelled to assume the characteristics of a political party. Unable to accomplish its goals within the system, Solidarity asked for free elections. Free elections, however, in Poland or any other Soviet bloc state would have conflicted with the division of Europe as provided by the 1945 Yalta agreement signed by Soviet Russia, the United States, and Great Britain.

The military regime's patriotic and other altruistic motives were questioned by two prominent Polish diplomats who defected to the United States following General Jaruzelski's war against the Polish nation. Romuald Spasowski, Polish ambassador to the United States, and Zdzisław Rurarz, Polish ambassador to Japan, asked for political asylum in Washington. In his testimony to a congressional commission, Rurarz described the Polish government as "in fact a Soviet fifth column . . . People are being denied the most basic human rights in the best fascist and Stalinist tradition."[21] Both men advised the U.S. authorities to impose an economic boycott on Poland and the Soviet Union. "Please do not give a single penny to the perfidious Polish junta," Rurarz asked before the U.S. Congress.[22]

The United States government was well informed about General Jaruzelski's preparations for martial law, but this information was never passed to the leaders of Solidarity. Large but unarmed, the union became the easy prey of Polish security forces. Later the Polish regime accused Washington of duplicity toward its allies in Poland; and there is no doubt that the internal invasion was viewed in the United States as a lesser evil than a Soviet-led attack on Poland by Warsaw Pact forces. Once Moscow decided that Solidarity had to be eliminated, the United States decided to minimize the danger of civil war in Poland. The failure of martial law would serve as an invitation for Soviet troops to enter the country. Fully aware of the limits to its influence on the communist regimes in Poland and Moscow, Washington acquiesced to General Jaruzelski's actions. It was not the first time since the end of World War II that the West was forced to recognize the Soviet Union's protection of its interests by a variety of means, including armed invasions and coups d'état in Eastern Europe. Compared to some Soviet political practices, martial law should be considered as a fairly humane way of dealing with opposition.

Following the post–World War II division of Europe, the United States recognized Eastern Europe as being within the Soviet domain, which excluded direct U.S. involvement on behalf of subjugated nations. However, the Western powers never committed themselves to the notion that this region was incorporated into the Soviet state and never considered developments east of the Elbe as internal Soviet affairs. Soviet mistreatment of its satellites could have a negative effect on East-West relations. The NATO states were inclined to assist Poland as long as the Polish state acted according to the norms of behavior acceptable by international and domestic laws, but were not willing to underwrite a regime that, acting as a Soviet puppet, invaded its own people.

The United States' position regarding the martial law regime was elaborated by President Reagan in a speech delivered on 23 December 1981. Making clear the distinction between the Moscow-oriented communist regime on one hand and the Polish nation on the other, the Reagan administration imposed economic sanctions on Poland that included the suspension or termination of numerous agreements between the two countries. Among those agreements were most-favored-nation status for Poland, the use of U.S. airspace by commercial Polish aircraft, Polish fishing rights in U.S. coastal waters, and U.S. government–guaranteed credits. Humanitarian aid, however, delivered to private organizations in Poland and distributed directly to the Polish people was exempted from the sanctions. Lifting the U.S. sanctions was to be contingent on improvements in Poland's human rights record.

Polish and Soviet authorities responded immediately to President Reagan's Christmas address with a long list of accusations that focused on alleged U.S. interference in Poland's domestic affairs. The Soviet sources emphasized that the United States was consistently wrong in its assessment of the situation. The sources claimed that the Soviet generals stood behind the events in Poland, and announced that the Soviet Union was planning to invade the country. According to Moscow, the United States failed to find evidence that the Soviet Union was responsible for the military crackdown on Solidarity, and so proceeded to blackmail Poland by suspending economic relations. This punishing of the Polish people, the Soviets argued, constituted a "monstrous provocation" and revenge for the "fact that the majority of [the Polish people] have accepted the introduction of martial law in the country and are striving to normalize the situation."[23]

Like the Polish regime, the Soviet authorities viewed the U.S. sanctions as targeting the Polish nation rather than the military regime. It was considered a punitive act and an interference in Poland's internal affairs, because the United States had made normalization of its relations with Poland conditional on continued reforms and a sustained dialogue with the union. According to the Soviets, the Reagan administration "would be happier if Solidarity extremists and other antistate groupings in Poland continued their antigovernment activities in the future and hindered in all possible ways the normalization of the situation in the country."[24]

The Polish and Soviet authorities took the view that any attempts to influence Poland's internal development by propagating views that differed from the officially stated position constituted illegal Western interference in Poland's domestic affairs. Moscow assumed the role of a guarantor of Poland's independence and a protector of the socialist domestic order supposedly preferred by a majority of the Poles. The purpose of the orchestrated Polish-Soviet propaganda was to convince the Polish people and Western public opinion that Solidarity was not an indigenous social movement in Poland, but rather a U.S. fifth column seeking the overthrow of communism. The United States, according to this view, was politically and morally responsible for everything that had happened in Poland, and the U.S. economic sanctions were pointed to as evidence of an anti-Polish U.S. policy.

The Polish and Soviet leaders used the U.S. policy toward the Polish martial-law regime as a scapegoat for their political and economic failures. Anti-Americanism became the key element in the political legitimization of Jaruzelski's regime. Since the military junta in Poland could not have the United States pay for its economic failures, it decided to justify its power with the help of a policy that portrayed the United States as a predatory superpower playing the Polish card at the expense of the Polish people to achieve a geostrategic victory over the Soviet Union.

The propaganda apparatus in Warsaw and Moscow capitalized on a statement by Secretary of State Alexander Haig, reported in the 27 December 1981 *Washington Post*. Haig had stated that the events in Poland had "historical importance" not only for the Polish nation but for the entire post–World War II international system. In Moscow, this statement was seized on as evidence of a capitalist plot to alter the balance of power and restore capitalism in Poland, a plot in which Solidarity played an important role "in the great political game of the enemies of peace and socialism."[25]

The Polish interpretation of the U.S. role in the crisis over the Solidarity union differed from the Soviet line only in nuance. While Moscow described martial law as enthusiastically welcomed and supported by the majority of the Polish population—and particularly the working class— General Jaruzelski chose to call it "a lesser evil than a fratricidal conflict which until recently was knocking on our door . . . There have been many moments in the history of Poland when the choice was not between good and evil but between greater and lesser evil. We have made this choice. I am confident that the future will pass a fair judgment on this choice."[26] According to his logic, the United States was behind the forces that pushed Poland toward the "greater evil."

As on many previous occasions, the Polish nation was caught between its own pro-Western, prodemocratic inclinations and the harsh political reality. Once again Poland was denied the right to self-determination and forced to serve the global ambitions of Soviet Russia. The Poles believed that Poland was "sentenced to communism" at the Yalta conference in 1945, and that General Jaruzelski's coup in December 1981 reaffirmed preference of the Big Three.

Following the destruction of Solidarity, U.S. policy toward Poland revolved around two principles: first, the internationalization of the Polish affair, which included directly accusing Moscow of orchestrating another brutal suppression of Poland's attempted emancipation from its imperial rule; and second, the dualism in U.S. relations with Poland, which differentiated between contacts with the Warsaw regime and ties with the Polish people. Washington, in effect, reversed its bridge-building policy of the 1970s, when the communist regime received full credit as a legitimate representation of the Polish nation. That assumption lost its validity when, after 35 years of communist rule, the Polish nation was "reconquered" rather than permitted to make its own free choice.

CHAPTER FOUR

Economic Sanctions

Until martial law was imposed in Poland, the United States emphasized the internal character of Polish developments, and consequently championed the principle of Polish sovereignty. That principle was brought into question by martial law, and the Reagan administration focused its attention on the Soviet Union as the true cause of the repression in Poland. Speaking on 29 December 1981 in Los Angeles, President Reagan decided to supplement economic sanctions against Jaruzelski's Poland with sanctions against the Soviet Union. The United States suspended Aeroflot's flights to the United States, closed the Soviet economic commission, suspended the licensing of electronic equipment and oil drilling equipment, suspended negotiations for long-term export of American grain to the Soviet Union, and terminated U.S.-Soviet negotiations on the access of each country's commercial ships to the other's ports.[1]

In addition, the United States called a special NATO session on 11 January 1982, in which all members agreed to condemn the Polish military and the Soviet Union for introducing martial law, and appealed to the Polish leaders to restore civil liberties and resume relations with the church and with Solidarity. The Western states agreed to condemn the Polish and Soviet authorities for violating the Helsinki Accord, and to restrict the movements of Polish and Soviet diplomats on Western territories. Although the NATO countries failed to agree on economic sanctions against Poland and the Soviet Union, the NATO declaration recognized the significance of the U.S. sanctions and promised to limit scientific and technological ties with the Soviet-bloc states.[2]

United States policy at the time had two objectives. First, sanctions against Jaruzelski's Poland and against Moscow were intended to apply economic pressure to the entire Soviet bloc, which was already experiencing severe economic difficulties. The Polish economy was in an especially critical situation and would require enormous hard-currency investments to recover from the crisis. The Western states were willing to assist Poland independently from the Soviet Union, but rejected Polish appeals to underwrite the unpopular pro-Soviet regime. Continuing subsidies for Poland were unacceptable to the Western public, and because of martial law, the Soviet Union had to assume full economic responsibility for its satellite.

The second U.S. policy objective was to use its economic leverage to press the military regime in Warsaw toward moderation and dialogue. Jaruzelski's government was considered an international outcast comparable to the most unpopular and brutal regimes in Latin America, such as Chile. International isolation and harsh criticism frustrated Jaruzelski's efforts to gain acceptance among the Polish people and to shake off his image as a Soviet general in Polish uniform.

The United States' diplomatic dualism toward Poland was the beginning of a long-term policy to exploit the internal division of the country. By supplementing its formal ties to the unpopular Polish government with a direct channel to the Polish people, the United States hoped to maintain contact with the Polish nation and to avoid seeming to conspire with Jaruzelski against the people. Washington decided to extend humanitarian aid to the Polish people independently from the regime in Warsaw. This decision was the first step of what eventually developed into a complex and mutually beneficial relationship that sustained the United States' image as a country concerned about the fate of the Polish nation. The isolation of the martial law regime did not isolate the Polish people from the democratic West.

This U.S. policy ran counter to the Polish-Soviet argument that what Polish authorities do to their own subjects is entirely a domestic matter. An interpretation of internal affairs that differed from the officially stated view came to be seen as a violation of Poland's sovereignty, as did the economic sanctions imposed by the United States against the Polish government. The Warsaw regime claimed that the United States had a legal and moral obligation to provide economic aid to the Polish authorities regardless of what they did to their own people. This opinion was officially expressed in the note sent by the Polish government to the U.S. government on 3 November 1983, in which Warsaw argued that martial law in Poland was not directed against any foreign government or state, including the United States, and was necessitated by progressing anarchy, destabilization of governmental structures, and the need to avoid civil war. Economic sanctions imposed on Poland, the note continued, violated numerous bilateral agreements, and Washington's willingness to lift the sanctions if civil rights were respected was criticized as attaching political conditions to economic relations.[3]

The essence of the Polish argument was political, not legal. The communist authorities were humiliated at home by Solidarity and internationally by the Western sanctions and by their dependence on Moscow. Jaruzelski and his group of generals were seen in the West as Soviet tools with little legitimacy. The U.S. policy exposed to world opinion the artificial nature of Poland's communist regime, and hindered the Poles' acceptance of military rule. The political implications of Western sanctions were the most irritating consequence of the U.S. policy, particularly because the great majority of Polish people supported the U.S. decision. Without Western economic and political support, martial law became a permanent feature of the Polish internal order. The Polish state assumed a repressive character and guided its foreign policy by the principle of "internalization" of Polish affairs. Having no substantive arguments to present for its defense, the Warsaw regime used narrowly constructed legalisms and accusations of an "anticommunist crusade" to defend itself against Western pressure.[4] As a result, Warsaw's highly defensive and emotional response to the Western sanctions contributed to the isolation and insecurity of the military junta.

The rupture of U.S.-Polish relations that was triggered by martial law and economic sanctions initiated a rapid disengagement of the United States from internal developments in Poland. Still, the Reagan administration's considerable restraint made Warsaw hopeful that an improvement in relations was possible. The real test of Reagan's long-term intentions toward Poland came at the beginning of February 1982, when the United States had to decide whether to pay $71.3 million in interest to U.S. banks that had made government-guaranteed loans to Poland. Several senators, including Patrick Moynihan, argued in favor of declaring Poland bankrupt. Such a decision would eliminate Polish exports to the West and make the Jaruzelski regime a financial ward of Moscow. This step would be the ultimate form of economic pressure on Warsaw and Moscow.[5]

The Reagan administration, however, believed that declaring Poland insolvent would have irreversible consequences on Polish-U.S. relations. This point was strongly emphasized by the United States' West European allies. The declared Western policy was to limit action against Poland to economic pressure in the form of an embargo on new credits. Declaring the country bankrupt would exceed the policy objectives stated by the West, and would offer the martial law regime no incentives to alter its policies. The United States favored a flexible approach to Poland—a policy of carrots and sticks—even if that involved paying Jaruzelski's debts.

The decision not to declare Poland bankrupt was a clear message to Warsaw that mutual relations were not beyond repair, and that the key to Poland's access to Western markets and credits was in General Jaruzelski's hands. It is next to impossible to determine to what extent the Jaruzelski regime exercised restraint toward the opposition in Poland as a result of U.S. pressure and in the hope that lucrative economic relations with the West would eventually be restored. During the next few years, however, the Polish regime repeatedly requested that the U.S. economic sanctions be lifted, and General Jaruzelski insisted that the timing of numerous domestic steps was dictated by an expected early lifting of the sanctions. However, Jaruzelski underestimated how serious the Reagan administration was about pressing Poland to end repressive policies. He also failed to realize that his policies would be judged by much higher standards than Czechoslovakia's so-called normalization after the Soviet invasion in 1968.

The U.S.-Polish rift over martial law also had its theatrical aspect. The United States government produced a television program entitled "Let Poland Be Poland," which was made available for foreign and domestic broadcasting. The Polish authorities, in retaliation, organized several conferences on the alleged CIA subversion in Poland. Invited guests, who included a number of foreign correspondents, were shown several films that, according to Warsaw, depicted espionage activities conducted on Polish territory by U.S. agents and the CIA's recruitment of Polish citizens traveling abroad. Special attention was placed on the alleged contacts between U.S. diplomats stationed in Poland and the Solidarity leadership. Solidarity's political successes were attributed to the activities of U.S. special services in Poland. Material collected by counterintelligence units of the Polish Ministry of Internal Affairs was presented as evidence of CIA-Solidarity collaboration to seize power in Poland.[6]

These shows consisted of crude fabrications and unsubstantiated allegations, with no logical relationship between the films, photographs, and equipment produced by the Polish authorities and the conclusions drawn by the Polish security forces. The shows merely discredited the military junta in the eyes of the public opinion at home and abroad. At the same time, these propaganda tricks intimidated the majority of Poles against seeking contacts with U.S. tourists and diplomats, because even the most casual encounter could result in accusations of espionage. Western academic, cultural, and charitable organizations were portrayed as centers of subversive activities directed against Poland. As characterized by the official sources, the anti-Polish campaign orchestrated and supervised by the CIA was more global in scope and more intense than any since 1945. Accepting any gifts, scholarships, and the like automatically made a Polish citizen suspect of being involved in subversive activities. In fact, the main objective of these shows may have been to discourage Polish citizens from making contact with foreigners and discussing the internal situation in Poland. The Warsaw regime was particularly apprehensive about what Polish nationals might say at the Madrid meeting to discuss the Helsinki Final Act that was scheduled for early February 1982.

Anti-U.S. propaganda in Poland became surprisingly crude, attacking not only Radio Free Europe but also the *Christian Science Monitor* and *Time* magazine as instruments of a "CIA spiderweb spreading all over the world, the purpose of which is to fight real socialism, the national liberation movement, the communist parties, the ideas of social progress and national liberation, and, in consequence, to ensure hegemony for American imperialism." The Western mass media and their representatives in Poland were labeled "agent-journalists" tasked with anti-Polish and anti-communist counterrevolutionary activity.[7]

In effect, General Jaruzelski's regime declared a propaganda war against the entire world, except for the regime's patrons in Moscow. The Soviet-bloc media attacked every independent publication critical of the regime's activities. Especially harsh was the criticism of West European communist parties that condemned Moscow for its policy of blocs and for its desire to defend its spheres of influence. The magazine *Novo vremyé*, for example, asked the Italian communist party how it could have "the audacity to come out against those actions of the USSR that have served and are serving as a guarantee against the export of counterrevolution, that are against crude attempts by the imperialist bloc to break down and alter in its own favor the relationship of forces that has arisen in the world and that are against attempts to turn back the process of social and political changes in the life of the people."[8] The Soviets' responsibility for martial law in Poland is implied in this statement.

During the first few months after the introduction of martial law, the political situation in Poland was unclear, as was the direction of future developments. Continuing political repression would be counterproductive in the long run, because without public support the military regime would never have a chance to rebuild Poland's economy. About 60 percent of Poland's entire labor force joined the Solidarity union, and it was up to them to decide Poland's economic and social future. Solidarity's main question concerned its legal future. The martial law regime arrested

Solidarity's top leadership and charged its members with treason, subversion, and counterrevolution. But the regime could not coerce more than ten million workers to work enthusiastically and productively. Moreover, the regime was bound (formally at least) by the August 1980 agreement and by the judicial authorities' decisions recognizing the union's legal existence. Although the union leadership was interned, the organization existed legally and continued to be backed by its members.

By internationalizing Poland's affairs and limiting the scope of the economic sanctions initially imposed by the Reagan administration, the United States intended to restrain Jaruzelski from putting Solidarity on trial and formally delegalizing the union. There was still some hope that the Polish authorities would permit Solidarity to have a limited, nonpolitical role. In addition, it was reasonable to expect that the Warsaw regime might be reluctant to hand down stiff sentences for the arrested activists of the opposition, as had been done under Kádár in Hungary and Husák in Czechoslovakia. The United States hoped for some modus vivendi between the party and the union, some form of coexistence like that between the party and the church in Poland. Washington was equally concerned about the fate of the interned leaders. Soviet pressure to treat them as foreign agents could lead to mass purges. The United States still held two powerful economic weapons aimed at Jaruzelski's regime: suspending Poland's most-favored-nation status and, as demanded by several leaders of the U.S. Senate, declaring Poland bankrupt, thus effectively terminating economic relations between Warsaw and the West.

The United States' pressure on Poland and the Soviet Union focused on world public opinion, which was frequently reminded of the fate of the Polish nation. Speaking at the Madrid meeting of the Conference on Security and Cooperation in Europe, Secretary of State Alexander Haig stated that the United States would not permit Warsaw and Moscow to place the "Polish tragedy outside the framework of the [Helsinki] Final Act."[9]

This point of view was reiterated frequently by U.S. diplomats before various United Nations committees and at the U.N. General Assembly, where Haig's successor as secretary of state, George Shultz, placed the Polish question among the top problems that were poisoning relations between East and West.[10] Polish, Soviet, and other Eastern-bloc representatives repeatedly insisted that Poland's martial law was a purely domestic issue, and that the United States' preoccupation with Polish affairs was a political maneuver intended to divert attention from disarmament and other peace-related issues. Soon it became obvious that the Soviets would not yield to world public opinion, and that the Polish government would attempt to eliminate Solidarity. The prospect of additional U.S. sanctions against Poland and the Soviet Union became more real.

The decision to replace Solidarity with a completely new trade union was formally made by the Polish parliament on 8 October 1982—ten months after martial law was imposed. Originally, the union was only suspended by the military regime, and the promised normalization implied that a dialogue between the communist authorities and the union would ensue. Whether in jail or underground, Solidarity's leaders repeatedly voiced a desire to negotiate with General Jaruzelski. The Warsaw regime had, in essence, three choices regarding the future of Solidarity. First, the union could be dissolved and replaced by another organization totally subservient to the party. Second, Solidarity could be revived under a new charter that would accept two basic canons of communist supremacy in Poland, namely the leading role of the party and, as top priority, friendship with the Soviet Union. Third, the authorities could postpone a decision about the union for several years, until the social and economic situation could stabilize and open more options.

The second choice, which would give Solidarity some independence in social and economic matters but distance it from politics, was preferred by the great majority of Poles and probably by the martial law authorities. After all, as Poland's trade union minister, Józef Ciosek, admitted, the choice was between legalizing Solidarity and finding $28 billion (the amount of Poland's foreign debt), "but no one would want to do this deal with us, especially not American businessmen."[11]

Not only were economic relations with the West at stake; the credibility of the Jaruzelski regime was on the line. The pronounced purpose of martial law was limited to excluding the so-called extremist, and not the authentic, representation of the Polish workers from the political scene. Eliminating the union altogether would reinforce Jaruzelski's image as a Soviet puppet and enormously complicate his task of bringing about economic recovery. The final judgment of Solidarity's fate was most likely made by the ailing Leonid Brezhnev. Moscow had argued for more than two years that Solidarity was a counterrevolutionary spearhead of U.S. imperialism. The union's continuing existence, even under a new charter accepted by the authorities, would set an unwelcome precedent of concessions extracted by the workers from their communist rulers. Solidarity damaged Moscow's reputation for invincibility and the communist party's legitimacy as the sole representation of the working class. Solidarity had become a symbol of resistance to communist rule.

Solidarity continued to appeal for dialogue. In the summer of 1982, for example, a Solidarity statement addressed to the government expressed remarkable political restraint. As a precondition for negotiations, the union accepted two founding principles of communist Poland: "Solidarity has not been and does not wish to be a political party. It has not been and does not want to be an anti-party, anti-government, anti-Socialist, and anti-Soviet organization . . . We are realistic and we are for Poland's participation in existing alliances. We realize that any effort to change them would mean conflict on a world scale . . . We want to be an independent, self-managing trade union."[12]

The regime, however, preferred to charge Solidarity with instigating internal conflicts, setting up an underground movement, and permitting the "workers' initiatives" to be "intercepted by the opposition forces from the outside so that the workers' political struggle may be exploited to undermine the foundations of the system."[13] Finally, the regime officially outlawed Solidarity. It was replaced with a completely new union. This step, even more than the implementation of martial law, marked a turning point in U.S.-Polish relations. Mutual hostility between Warsaw and Washington set in.

Relations between the two countries continued to deteriorate. Bitter and unrestrained anti-U.S. propaganda prevailed in the official Polish press. The regime in Warsaw had a difficult time controlling public demonstrations, and needed a scapegoat to take the blame for the nation's unrest. Following the clashes between supporters of Solidarity and internal security forces at the beginning of May 1982, the Polish authorities staged a KGB-like setup. Two U.S. diplomats were accused of possessing written materials described by the Polish press agency as "hitting out at the interests of the Polish People's Republic."

Poland's foreign ministry did not present any papers seized by the police, nor were the charges substantiated in any other way. The U.S. diplomats, John Jerolis (the scientific and technical affairs officer) and James Howard (the first secretary for cultural affairs), were treated brutally by the plainclothes police, accused of engaging in activities inconsistent with their diplomatic status, declared to be personae non gratae, and expelled from Poland. The United States protested, stating, "We categorically reject the charges of the Ministry of Foreign Affairs that the two officers named were engaged in activities, as the ministry put it, prejudicial to the process of stabilization in the Polish state."[14]

The immediate cause of the Polish setup was, most likely, the United States' unwillingness to sign an agreement to finance scientific projects in Poland, which was negotiated before martial law was imposed. Following the incident, the U.S. State Department expelled two Polish diplomats from the United States and suspended travel financing for Polish and U.S. scientists conducting research funded by the United States. Clearly, Polish-

U.S. relations became confrontational once the military authorities in Warsaw concluded that they had nothing to lose. Poland's policy toward the United States was managed to suit the regime's domestic political needs, and particularly to provide justification for the regime's activities against Polish society and to remove any doubts about Poland's loyalty to the Soviet Union.

Domestic pressure in the United States to impose tougher sanctions on Poland increased, reflecting the American public's frustration over Jaruzelski's belligerent dealings with the United States and his heavy-handed treatment of Solidarity. The AFL-CIO and the Polish-American Congress in the United States were particularly active in support of a total economic embargo on Poland and other Soviet-bloc states. On 18 June 1982, President Reagan issued an embargo on deliveries of U.S.-made equipment for the Siberian pipeline, which was to provide Soviet natural gas for Western Europe. The president also prohibited U.S. companies and their foreign subsidiaries and affiliates from exporting high technology to Soviet-bloc countries. The goal of these sanctions was to prevent the Soviet Union from using Western technology to construct the 2,600-mile pipeline. However, owing to bitter opposition from West European leaders, the ban on exporting high technology was eased on 13 November. The Reagan administration explained that its purpose had been to demonstrate American displeasure with Soviet actions in Poland. The high-tech exports were allowed to continue, but under strict scrutiny on a case-by-case basis.

The Soviet leaders were again charged with direct responsibility for the political crisis in Poland. The United States could see no reason for assisting Moscow and its East European clients in overcoming their economic difficulties. The Polish government had become a Soviet tool, and Moscow was told to accept full financial responsibility for Poland's economic woes. On 9 October 1982, the day after the Polish parliament disbanded Solidarity, President Reagan suspended Poland's most-favored-nation status. This step increased tariffs on Polish products exported to the United States by 300 to 400 percent, making them unattractive for U.S. customers. Poland lost its lucrative U.S. markets and the political prestige associated with U.S. trade.

In a radio address to the nation on Solidarity and U.S. relations with Poland, President Reagan stated:

> Ever since martial law was brutally imposed last December, Polish authorities have been assuring the world that they're interested in a genuine reconciliation with the Polish nation. But the Polish regime's action yesterday reveals the hollowness of its promises. By outlawing Solidarity, a free trade organization to which an overwhelming majority of Polish

workers and farmers belong, they have made it clear that they never had any intention of fostering one of the most elementary human rights—the right to belong to a free trade union.

The president concluded: "Surely, it must be clear to all that until Warsaw's military authorities move to restore Solidarity to its rightful and hard-won place in Polish society, Poland will continue to be plagued by bitterness, alienation, instability, and stagnation."[15]

The Polish regime immediately responded by again accusing the United States of a "brutal" interference in Poland's domestic affairs and a breach of international agreements between the countries. Warsaw argued that the Reagan administration was punishing the Polish nation for refusing to play a role in its "anticommunist crusade," by "discriminating" against their country and lowering its standard of living.[16] The charge of discrimination was a direct response to the Reagan administration's suspension of Poland's trading status. The administration used as a pretext Poland's failure to increase its total value of imports from other GATT member nations by at least 7 percent per year for four years, as stipulated by the general terms of trade among the members. Poland was not the only member of GATT unable to meet this obligation, but Washington used this failure to deny Poland most-favored-nation trading status, which guarantees favorable tariff treatment.

Freeing Solidarity leader Lech Wałęsa from internment was Warsaw's feeble attempt to show its concern for human rights and to demonstrate how quickly the country could return to normality. The military regime was losing credibility in the international arena, but it was gaining confidence at home. Its brutal tactics began to pay dividends as the Polish people grew intimidated by the mass arrests, occasional killings, and heavy fines for participation in political protests. There were mass demonstrations on 31 August 1982 to commemorate the second anniversary of Solidarity's formation, and strikes on 11–12 October 1982 to protest the banning of Solidarity. The public participation in these events was large but not overwhelming, a sign that the Polish people were exhausted and disinclined to fight further. General Jaruzelski quickly shifted gears and offered several "carrots," among them an announcement that Pope John Paul II would visit Poland in June 1983. On the first anniversary of the declaration of martial law, the Polish authorities promised to ease some restrictions, including wiretapping of telephone conversations, censorship of mail, and restrictions on domestic travel; they also promised to release a large number of political prisoners.

General Jaruzelski's 12 December 1982 speech to the Polish nation sounded triumphant. He claimed to have won "a war for preserving and continuity of the socialist statehood" and praised the nation for the "patriotism of the society, wisdom, the attitude of the working class, [which] made it that the enemy's calls went unheeded." To the United States he said: "We have survived the boycott, restrictions and the barrage of an instigatory propaganda. The government of the United States and some of its customers could see for themselves the evidence of bankruptcy of the attempts to interfere in Polish internal affairs. The Polish destinies are being decided only here, on the Vistula and Odra rivers." This attack on Washington was followed by flattering remarks for the Soviets, for their "assistance" during the difficult days. The general condemned the United States for supporting the Polish nation in this struggle against communism, and acclaimed Moscow for suppressing freedom in Poland. Unfortunately, one cannot agree with Jaruzelski that a "new period [was] beginning in the life of Poland."[17]

Jaruzelski's talk of liberalization and his promises to develop "independent, self-governing trade unions" to replace Solidarity had no effect on Western perceptions of the Polish situation. Previously hailed by the West as the most independent member of the Warsaw Pact and as having a moderating influence on Moscow, Poland was rapidly declining in economic significance. Western sympathy and admiration for the Polish people remained strong, but the economic prospects of the Polish state had darkened, discouraging investments and deterring trade. Breaking out of international isolation became Warsaw's main foreign policy objective, but Poland's attempts to regain its international position were severely handicapped by domestic instability and by the regime's continuing use of coercive measures.

The delegalization of Solidarity triggered cold war–like relations between Poland and the United States. Poland's ceaseless attacks on the United States became the main ingredients of General Jaruzelski's *Westpolitik*—a peculiar way to resist international isolation and attract Washington's attention. The ruling junta in Warsaw apparently had concluded that a bad press would be better than no press at all. Having nothing to lose, it mounted an unprecedented anti-U.S. campaign designed to demonstrate that Poland could stand up to the superpower. Ironically, the Polish authorities simultaneously demanded that the United States immediately lift its economic sanctions, and make new credits available for the floundering Polish economy. America's "imperialist sanctions" were, according to the Polish authorities, the leading cause of Poland's economic crisis.

General Jaruzelski's new accusations had appeared for the first time in a speech to Polish miners delivered on 3 December 1982. In that speech he charged the United States with attempting to eliminate Poland as an economic competitor, claiming that it was typical capitalist greed that permeated the United States' actions against Poland. The United States, in his opinion, wished to "paralyze and starve" Poland, to "break down the energy-producing industries," and thus lower foreign competition for its own companies.[18]

Warsaw began to argue that the economic sanctions imposed by the United States against Jaruzelski's regime were responsible for the economic and social crisis, which the military regime was incapable of harnessing. According to the studies commissioned by the Polish government, American economic restrictions against Poland had two negative effects. First, the international consequences of the U.S. policy toward Poland were a deterioration in East-West relations, and a higher-risk climate for East-West trade. Second, scientific and technological cooperation between Poland and the United States had suffered since the U.S. government decided to halt financing of scientific projects by Polish scientists.

These losses, which according to Polish authorities were impossible to calculate, were in addition to the macroeconomic sanctions imposed by Washington. It was estimated that those sanctions had cost the national economy $7.1 billion in 1981, $5.1 billion in 1982, and $0.3 billion in 1983—a total of $12.5 billion in three years, amounting to approximately $350 per capita over the three-year period.[19] These losses were ascribed to the cutoff of American credits and the drastic reduction of imports from the West and of hard-currency exports.

The formula for calculating this $12.5 billion reduction in Poland's gross national product was highly subjective and self-serving. The authors of the estimate completely ignored the crisis conditions of the Polish economy that had paralyzed real growth before the emergence of Solidarity in August 1980. Members of the Institute on Contemporary Problems of Capitalism in Warsaw had expected the Polish economy to grow at an unrealistic annual rate of about 3 percent in the absence of Western economic sanctions. Equally unrealistic was the assumption that Polish exports to the West would grow by at least 4.5 percent per year. Moreover, the rate of exchange between the Polish zloty and the U.S. dollar was artificially set at 90 to 1. Based on these assumptions, the Polish authorities advanced the totally unsubstantiated argument that the direct cause of Poland's hardships was the capitalist West, and particularly the United States, rather than the communist party–controlled Polish economic system.

Polish attacks on the United States and several other Western countries coincided with an effort to complete the pacification of the Polish nation and proclaim an end to martial law. At the end of 1982, martial law was officially suspended, and the Polish authorities dispatched Deputy Foreign Minister Jan Kinast to Washington to negotiate the lifting of at least some economic sanctions and, above all, to restore the most-favored-nation status for Poland. His mission failed. The internal turmoil in Poland continued and the heavily armed security forces of the Interior Ministry were frequently deployed to break up peaceful strikes and demonstrations. The regime's reliance on raw physical power had not diminished. Suspending martial law made no difference in Poland's human rights situation. The restrictions introduced under martial law had been incorporated into Polish legislation, and many political prisoners were still behind bars. By suspending martial law the Polish authorities were only pretending that positive changes were taking place in the country.

The United Nations Human Rights Commission received a report on the Polish situation at the beginning of 1983. Prepared by U.N. under secretary-general Hugo Gobbi, this document accused the Polish regime of serious human rights violations. More than six thousand Solidarity leaders were forcibly detained during the initial phase of martial law, and at least nine people died during police attacks on mines and factories. Police brutality, even murders, became common. The only satisfaction the Polish regime could derive from the Gobbi report was the statement that in declaring martial law the government acted within its constitutional power. However, the report noted that trade union pluralism, recognized as a universal human right, was seriously violated by the military authorities. The report's conclusions were, as expected, rejected by the Polish authorities. In fact, the Polish delegate to the Human Rights Commission claimed that no foreign state had the right to assess Poland's internal situation in any way that would differ from the interpretation presented by the Polish government. Poland rejected the U.S. resolution that was based on the report, dismissing it as a flagrant example of interference in the country's internal affairs, and claiming that it was an "illegal, invalid, politically harmful and morally two-faced" orchestration of U.S. policy.[20]

Because little progress in human rights had been made in Poland by early 1983, the United States decided against concessions that would favor the Polish government. This hard-line policy aimed at Warsaw's military junta was strongly supported by most Poles and openly advocated by Solidarity leader Lech Wałęsa. Similar attitudes prevailed among the American public. For example, the AFL-CIO issued another appeal in favor of a strict economic blockade of Poland and the Soviet Union, and demanded that Poland be declared bankrupt.[21] The American union was protesting the delegalization of Solidarity and its replacement by new trade unions subordinated to the regime.

The U.S. policy of economic sanctions, which denied the Polish regime access to Western credits, technology, animal fodder, and hard-currency earnings, might have been popular in Poland and the United States, but the authorities in Warsaw calculated that the United States eventually would have to reverse its stance. The authorities believed that the relative importance of Poland within the Soviet bloc and in Europe was too significant for the United States to be able to ignore Poland's rulers—no matter who they might be. The balance of power between NATO and the Warsaw Pact countries was directly affected by the Polish situation. The uncertainty of martial law and the prolonged conflict with the opposition had had a destabilizing effect on the entire European continent. The Polish regime expected that, sooner or later, perhaps under West European pressure, the United States would reverse its policy, since its net international effect was adverse to the vital strategic interests of the West. Isolated from the United States and the key states of Western Europe as a result of the sanctions, Poland was rapidly losing its traditionally semi-independent status vis-à-vis Moscow.

The U.S. economic restrictions aimed at the military regime also had a very painful effect on the Polish standard of living. The quality of life in Poland was declining at more than 20 percent annually, and the generous humanitarian aid provided by Western nations for the Polish people could never make up for the 50 to 60 percent reduction in Poland's industrial production. General Jaruzelski and his advisors knew that the old Leninist principle "the worse the better" was working to their advantage. At some point, ideological and political differences would cease to matter, and out of sheer physical necessity the Poles and their genuine representatives, such as the Catholic church and Solidarity, would use their influence in the West to lift the economic restrictions.

Poland's policy toward the United States was one of wait-and-see, augmented by a well-advertised integration into the Soviet bloc and unusually strong support for Moscow's foreign policy against the United States. On many occasions, foreign policy statements delivered by the Polish government resembled a translation from the Russian, or even exceeded Soviet rhetoric in anti-U.S. pronouncements.

The anti-Polish campaign that the regime attributed to the U.S. government could not sound plausible to the Polish people; the regime therefore alleged that the Reagan administration's anticommunist crusade was harming the Polish nation. It was neither new nor originally a Polish idea to place Western sanctions against Poland in the broader international context and argue that the entire U.S. foreign policy was obsessed with a bellicose "missile philosophy." Keeping up domestic tensions in Poland was supposed to serve the United States' drive to deploy nuclear cruise and Pershing II missiles in Western Europe. Political tensions in Europe and worsening East-West relations, the Polish authorities argued, facilitated the implementation of the U.S. plan to place new missiles on the

European continent.[22] Poland, according to the Polish authorities, was used by the United States to shift the balance of power in Europe; and the deployment of the new U.S. weapons was allegedly facilitated by continuing instability in Poland. The logical conclusion of this officially advanced argument was that to support U.S. economic sanctions against the Polish regime was automatically to support nuclear weapons aimed at Polish territory. Speaking at the meeting of trade union activists in Katowice on 20 August 1983, General Jaruzelski stated that "Poland has become a kind of pretext for cold war forces, for destabilization forces; it has become an instrument that people have attempted to play on to justify different kinds of steps harmful to international relations." "Poland," he said, "appeared to be an excellent argument for nuclear armaments."[23]

In fact, Warsaw was becoming an obedient tool in Soviet foreign policy. Denied access to Western markets, the Polish government implemented comprehensive structural changes in the export sector of the national economy. The geographic orientation of Polish foreign trade moved away from the highly industrialized Western democracies back to integration into the Soviet-bloc states and cartel-like cooperation with underdeveloped Third World countries. The United States was losing its influence on Poland. As General Jaruzelski phrased it, the Reagan administration "evacuated" itself from Poland.[24] Jaruzelski's Poland was moving back to a pre-détente, one-sided foreign policy, abandoning the more balanced outlook of the 1970s. The official Polish view of the sanctions was that they were keenly felt by the economy and resulted in enormous social hardship, but that they had become politically ineffective, if not counterproductive. In the official attitude, the Polish government would not be punished or blackmailed; only the Polish people would lose wages owing to the economic and political war launched by U.S. capitalism. An attempt to punish the government had the effect of punishing the people, whom the United States claimed it wished to protect.

By the end of 1983 it was obvious that the Western economic sanctions against the Polish regime were to continue longer than expected. Jaruzelski's political maneuvers included lifting martial law on 22 July, an amnesty for political prisoners, a visit by Pope John Paul II, and enactment of the law that, in the view of the Polish government, brought to life a free and independent union. The Warsaw authorities, claiming that Poland had fulfilled all the West's demands (short of dismantling the communist system), called for an immediate lifting of the economic restrictions. The West's unwillingness to recognize progress toward genuine normalization was again seen as an attempt to use the Polish card in the East-West strategic game, and a sign that bilateral relations between Poland and the Western countries were no longer possible.

In August 1983 U.S. senator Christopher Dodd, a member of the Senate Foreign Relations Committee and chairman of the International Financial and Monetary Policy Subcommittee, visited Poland to assess the internal situation and recommend the future course of U.S. policy toward Poland. The American politician was received by Janusz Obwodowski, deputy chairman of the Council of Ministers, and held talks with the Polish minister of finances and the acting head of the Foreign Ministry. As a result of those talks, Senator Dodd concluded that it would be premature to lift all sanctions immediately; instead he recommended a partial easing of some of the restrictions. The U.S. government subsequently recognized marginal improvements in Poland by lifting the ban on fishing off the U.S. coast. The United States would lift the remaining sanctions only if Solidarity's legal status was restored.

Dodd admitted that the Polish people were paying the consequences of the U.S. economic sanctions; but he was undoubtedly influenced by Lech Wałęsa's advice that the sanctions were still necessary. Wałęsa's opinion was based on the fact that there had been very little real progress in human rights in Poland. Furthermore, there were no guarantees that any newly borrowed capital could be repaid. Solidarity's position on new credits was to avoid a situation in which the regime could mishandle foreign money that Polish workers must repay. The regime, having failed to reestablish lucrative economic contacts with the West, used the occasion of Senator Dodd's visit to attack Wałęsa for his alleged anti-Polish, antiworker policies. He was declared to be a traitor, a "Yankee from Gdańsk" with whom negotiations would be useless.[25]

The Polish authorities understood that a permanent shift in the country's economic policy was unavoidable. The regime would not resume its dialogue with Solidarity, regardless of the socioeconomic consequences of the failure of national reconciliation. The authorities continued to insist that Solidarity was reduced to a handful of extremists who were out of touch with the Polish people. They further insisted that if the West intended to deal with Poland it had to address its communist government—on the political terms presented by the martial law authorities. Under no circumstances would the Polish authorities consider the legalization of Solidarity. On several occasions General Jaruzelski emphasized that there would be no return to the situation that existed before 13 December 1981.

On 3 November 1983, in a last-ditch effort to persuade the United States to lift its economic restrictions, the Polish government issued a lengthy note to the United States that carefully presented Poland's position on all issues of mutual concern. The note began with the assertion that the sanctions were "lawless measures," because the decision to introduce martial law was a sovereign decision of the Polish government, made within its constitutional powers. The purpose of martial law, according to the Polish authorities, was "to put a stop to anarchy and to prevent a fratricidal conflict, a collapse of the economy, and the destabilization of the state and social structure." Martial law "was not aimed against any state whatsoever," including the United States. On the contrary, martial law preserved stability in Europe in accordance with the spirit and letter of the Helsinki Accord. In this context, the U.S. policy toward Poland, that is, "the sudden blocking of previously arranged credits . . . resulted in a drop in production in many spheres, including [that] of supplies for the population . . . The restrictions and other hostile measures have affected the whole of Polish society, have caused Polish society's standard of living to drop, and have enhanced the burdens of daily life. All this has caused and is still causing serious losses for the Polish economy running into billions of dollars."

Referring to the political ramifications of the American policy, the note stated that

> The U.S. government's policy toward Poland constitutes impermissible interference in our state's domestic affairs, exerts pressure on Poland, and tries to impose on Poland political solutions that are contrary to the vital needs of national existence—while at the same time violating the sovereign rights of the Polish state . . . It is therefore clear that the real aim of the U.S. government's policy is to increase economic difficulties, sow social tension, encumber efforts at reaching national accord, and make it difficult to implement sociopolitical and economic reforms . . . The government of the Polish People's Republic has stated many times that it rejects and will continue to reject this kind of pressure, which is doomed to failure just like all other forms of pressure so far.[26]

This was the Polish way of informing the United States that the Polish authorities were unequivocally committed to preserving the communist political framework in Poland, regardless of the system's lack of popularity with the Poles or with foreign powers. Because Solidarity threatened Poland's existence as an independent state, it could never be given legal status again. The government's note ended with the expectation "that the U.S. government will take the necessary steps to remove the losses suffered by the Polish economy and people" to prevent the "further deterioration" of bilateral relations.[27]

Although the impact of this Polish note on relations with the United States was minimal, the Warsaw regime achieved a major success at home. Its businesslike approach to the economic sanctions and its skillful manipulation of the facts to imply that the United States should bear principal responsibility for Poland's economic hardship had a notable effect on the Polish public, which was tired of economic hardship. Two years after the declaration of martial law, the Poles turned from political matters to bread-and-butter issues; and once again they looked to the United States for economic assistance. After all, in the 1970s the West had agreed to cooperate with the communist authorities to benefit the Polish people. Since the Polish communist system could not be changed, the United States could return to the policy practiced during the era of détente. This change in the public mood, undoubtedly a sign of resignation and apathy, was noted by Solidarity. In early December 1983 Lech Wałęsa reversed his previous support for Western economic sanctions and appealed for economic help to ease the suffering of the Polish people. At this point the regime declared its victory over the United States and Solidarity. Jerzy Urban, spokesman for the Polish government, declared that the sanctions were politically counterproductive because they substantially decreased American influence in Poland. The United States, having failed to obtain the reinstatement of Solidarity, began to look for means to reestablish its influence in Polish politics. Wałęsa's appeal to the United States to lift the sanctions was described by Urban as a face-saving scheme to reverse a faulty policy.[28]

The gradual turnaround in U.S. policy toward Poland began late in 1983, when the internal situation stabilized and, following the visit by the pope, the regime emerged from its isolation. Moreover, it became obvious that the Polish regime had succeeded in its attempt to destroy the organizational structure of Solidarity but had failed to control internal developments in Poland. In the absence of Solidarity, Lech Wałęsa, who received the Nobel peace prize, became a symbol of opposition against the regime. Western sanctions had achieved the goal of preserving political pluralism in Poland; but to continue this policy could become counterproductive, hindering political and economic reforms and pushing the country toward greater dependence on Moscow.

Noting these "positive developments" and responding to Lech Wałęsa's appeal to ease the economic hardships suffered by the Polish people, in early 1984 President Reagan restored the right of Polish vessels to fish in U.S. waters and permitted 88 charter flights from Poland to the United States by the Polish national airline. The spokesman of the U.S. State Department, Alan Romberg, explained that it was "the President's hope that the Administration's action will help contribute to the process of reconciliation and the improvement of human rights in Poland." At the same time, the White House emphasized that "there's no change in policy."[29]

There was also no change in the regime's policy toward Polish society. The political atmosphere improved noticeably, but the post–martial law regime was still coercive. It harassed or banned numerous social organizations representing students, writers, journalists, and filmmakers, and the number of political prisoners grew from 161 in October 1983 to 652 in July 1984. The Catholic church, however, retained its autonomous political position, and Lech Wałęsa continued to speak freely on behalf of the Polish nation. The United States gave both the church and Wałęsa a significant role in determining Washington's policy of economic sanctions, thus sending a message to the ruling junta that additional restrictions would be repealed only if de facto pluralism and political tolerance were increased. The process of improving U.S.-Polish relations was carried out through a "small steps" policy that carefully calibrated U.S. actions to human rights improvements in Poland.

Warsaw hailed even this minor change in U.S. policy as a victory. The U.S. sanctions, according to Warsaw, had missed their intended target, and instead of hurting the regime they had caused serious harm to the nation. Lech Wałęsa, who on behalf of Solidarity had supported the U.S. sanctions, was proclaimed to be "an enemy of the fundamental interests of every family" in Poland.[30] General Jaruzelski concluded that the country "survived the economic blackmail, thanks mainly to the patriotic and devoted attitudes of our country's working class," and thanks to the assistance received from Moscow and other Soviet-bloc states.[31] The Reagan administration was held partly responsible for the country's increase in foreign debts, which by the end of 1983 amounted to approximately $26.4 billion. Once again the regime refused to admit that Poland's economic system and human rights violations were primarily responsible for the country's social and economic disorder.

While accusing the United States of such "crimes," the Polish regime failed to inform its countrymen that in 1984 U.S. taxpayers paid $941 million to U.S. banks on loans to Poland that were guaranteed by the U.S. government. Poland, while paying its financial obligations to private creditors in exchange for new credits, refused to honor U.S. government–guaranteed obligations. As a precondition for repaying any loans secured by the U.S. government, Poland demanded that the economic sanctions be lifted, that the most-favored-nation status be restored, and that government-to-government credits be granted.[32] This was the Polish way of exerting pressure on the United States to lift the sanctions and allow Poland to earn money by trading with the United States.

In order to show further progress toward full normalization, the Polish regime enacted another amnesty on 22 July 1984 that resulted in the release of almost all political prisoners. Apparently, the Poles were not obtaining sufficient economic aid from their Warsaw Pact allies, and therefore proceeded to please the West in hope of direct financial benefits. The amnesty was not accompanied by legalization of Solidarity—such a move would have been unacceptable to Moscow—but it created a new legal ground for the tolerance of political opposition.

Warsaw expected a quick response from Washington after the political prisoners were freed. The Poles hoped for a restoration of the most-favored-nation status, a U.S. government–guaranteed loan, and immediate approval for membership in the International Monetary Fund (IMF), which could have provided a loan of $3 to $4 billion within six months. The United States, however, decided to move slowly, only restoring U.S. landing rights for Polish commercial aircraft and lifting the ban on government-funded scientific exchanges organized by the Maria Skłodowska-Curie Foundation. President Reagan expressed hope that the United States could eventually remove its opposition to Polish membership in the IMF, provided that the amnesty was implemented faithfully.[33] No immediate, sweeping changes in U.S. policy toward Poland were contemplated; such changes could come only with restoration of the pre–martial law status quo in Poland.

The reaction in Warsaw reflected disappointment that the amnesty, a radical step that would obviously irritate the Soviets, received so little appreciation in Washington. The 6 August 1984 *Życie warszawy* demanded "full, quick, and unconditional removal of all discriminatory and hostile acts toward our country, giving up all kinds of interference in our internal affairs, respect of sovereignty, building mutual relations on the principle of full equality and respect for the partner, and finally—creating conditions for compensating us for the sustained losses." President Reagan's step-by-step approach to Poland was described as "an illusion that he is gradually withdrawing the restrictions."

The 40th anniversary of the Warsaw uprising provided another occasion for deepening the Polish-U.S. rift. President Reagan hosted representatives of Armia Krajowa (the Home Army) at a White House luncheon, presenting the Legion of Merit award to three prominent leaders of the Polish underground during World War II. These leaders, in Reagan's words, were "never given their due after the Allied victory" because the communist authorities refused to recognize the military contribution of the government-in-exile in London. In his lengthy statement, the President also made reference to the Yalta agreement, saying that

We reject any interpretation . . . that suggests American consent for the division of Europe into spheres of influence. On the contrary, we see that agreement as a pledge by the three great powers to restore full indepen-

dence and to allow free and democratic elections in all countries liber-
ated from the Nazis after World War II, and there is no reason to
absolve the Soviet Union or ourselves from this commitment. We shall
continue to press for full compliance with it, and with the Charter of the
United Nations, the Helsinki Final Act, and other international agreements guaranteeing fundamental human rights.[34]

A similar reference to the Yalta agreement was included in the President's political campaign speech in Doylestown, Pennsylvania. Addressing
a crowd of Polish-Americans, Reagan stated: "Let us not be tempted into
giving Yalta as coverage to those who have violated that agreement; that
agreement never gave them the power to dominate the countries of Eastern Europe and Poland as they have."[35]

Questioning the Soviet interpretation of the Yalta agreement was, for
the Polish regime, tantamount to undermining its legitimacy to govern the
Polish nation. For the communists in Warsaw, any alternative to the Soviet interpretation of the post–World War II settlement in Europe was
enough to trigger unrestrained verbal attack on the United States. General
Jaruzelski accused President Reagan of continuing the anticommunist crusade and treating all of Europe as a hostage in the United States' struggle
with the Soviet Union.[36] The Yalta agreement, in Jaruzelski's view, was
the basis for the postwar political and territorial order in Europe that
gave the communists power to rule in Poland.[37] Western doubts about
Yalta were seen as a sign of growing tensions between the superpowers.
Under such circumstances, the Polish authorities preferred to retreat to the
safe ground of pro-Soviet loyalty. In addition, the Poles knew that they
could expect very little progress in relations with the United States during
the 1984 U.S. presidential campaign. President Reagan's gesture to the
American voters of Polish origin inevitably involved condemnation, rather
than appeasement, of Warsaw.

Only minor improvements in U.S.-Polish relations were accomplished
by late 1985. On 11 October the countries concluded an agreement concerning the export of Polish textiles to the United States, and by the end
of the year Poland was informed that Washington would no longer object
to Polish membership in the IMF. Meanwhile, the United States continued
to provide direct economic aid to the Polish people, earmarking $30 mil-
lion in surplus food for fiscal year 1985.[38] (The United States distributed
more than $130 million in surplus food between 1982 and 1985.)

The slow improvement in relations came to a full stop in early 1985.
After three years of political accusations and economic disengagement,
both governments were left with relatively few links on which to recon-
struct old ties. In addition, Poland was losing its strategic importance as a

result of internal developments in Moscow. The end of the U.S. presidential campaign also contributed to the decline in U.S. interest in Poland. Meanwhile, the Polish authorities adopted a highly aggressive propaganda posture to communicate their displeasure with the Reagan administration's wait-and-see policy. This sudden swing to a hard-line position vis-à-vis the United States was accompanied by a fresh wave of attacks against Solidarity, the leaders of which were rearrested and put on trial for treason. The Polish mass media organized another campaign to represent Solidarity as a CIA offshoot.

The immediate cause for deteriorating relations was the program (in Polish) broadcast by Radio Free Europe on 7 January 1985, which compared General Jaruzelski's success in suppressing the Polish nation to Adolf Hitler's celebration of the Nazis' victory over Poland in November 1939. A few days later the Polish government turned down a U.S. offer to exchange ambassadors, characterizing the offer as an ultimatum. The Polish regime instead offered comprehensive negotiations on all aspects of mutual relations. Warsaw, deeply frustrated with the United States' small-steps policy, was demanding a general revision of the U.S. approach to Poland. The Polish regime's conditions were spelled out by General Jaruzelski in an interview published in the *Times of India,* in which he asked the United States to respect Poland's sovereignty—that is, to recognize the legitimacy of the Polish communist order and to refrain from interfering in Poland's internal affairs, which amounted to a request to stop applying a human rights standard to the regime's measures to suppress opposition. He also asked the United States to lift all remaining economic sanctions.[39]

Warsaw did not rely on political statements alone to attract Washington's attention. On 25 February 1985 Colonel Frederick Myer, a U.S. military attaché in Poland, and his wife were detained by Polish internal security forces and charged with espionage. Both were treated brutally, declared to be personae non gratae, and asked to leave Poland within 48 hours. Believing that the Polish security forces had provoked the incident, Washington retaliated by expelling Colonel Zygmunt Szymanski, a Polish military attaché in the United States, and recalling the chargé d'affaires at the U.S. embassy in Poland for consultation in Washington. The United States also suspended talks about renewing scientific exchanges.

This diplomatic skirmish had no effect, however, on the conclusion of a new civil aviation arrangement. A three-year contract normalizing scheduled and chartered flights was signed in Warsaw on 16 April. The Poles gained a long-term agreement in exchange for dropping claims against the United States for its unilateral suspension of the previous agreement.[40]

This positive development was countered by another provocation or-chestrated by Poland's internal security forces. Two American diplomats, William Harwood, a first secretary of the U.S. embassy in Warsaw, and David Hopper, the U.S. consul in Krakow, were accused of aggressive be-havior, including "chanting anti-state slogans, carrying banners with hostile inscriptions, and spreading leaflets" during an unauthorized dem-onstration. Both diplomats were detained, "pushed, struck, kicked, and forced" to enter police vehicles. The U.S. embassy in Poland denied the charges and accused the Poles of instigating an undesirable incident.[41] The two diplomats were expelled from Poland, and the U.S. government retaliated by expelling four Polish diplomats from the United States. Po-land, in turn, accused the United States of seeking revenge, and suspended the privilege of official diplomatic air courier flights between West Berlin and Warsaw. Justifying its actions, the Polish government cited the drastic reduction of U.S. diplomatic activities in Poland.[42]

Having hit bottom in their relations, the two governments concluded a new agreement on 1 August 1985 granting Poland the right to fish in U.S. coastal waters. Another positive step was Cardinal Glemp's visit to the United States in late September. He visited several major U.S. cities soliciting support for a Polish agricultural foundation and campaigning for the repeal of all economic sanctions, which he said had caused "great damage to the Polish people."[43] The United States government pledged $10 million in support for the foundation. There was no immediate ac-tion, however, regarding the economic sanctions.

The cardinal's official visit was followed by General Jaruzelski's ar-rival in New York to address the United Nations General Assembly on 27 September. After learning that no U.S. officials were to meet the arriv-ing head of state—as a gesture of protest against the growing number of Polish political prisoners—the general decided to retaliate by flying to New York from Havana and delivering an address at the United Nations that was highly critical of the United States.[44] Meanwhile, the Polish government accused the Reagan administration of "bad manners" and as-sailed the White House statement praising Solidarity on the fifth anniver-sary of the Gdańsk agreement.[45]

Ignored by the Reagan administration, the Polish delegation met with David Rockefeller; Zbigniew Brzezinski, President Carter's national secu-rity adviser; and Lawrence Eagleburger, the under secretary of state for political affairs, to discuss a church-sponsored proposal to promote an agricultural foundation in Poland with the $300 million in assistance pro-vided by the Rockefeller Foundation.[46] These talks failed to produce any tangible results.

There was no sympathy for the Jaruzelski regime in the West. The general was never able to project the image of a Polish patriot who saved his nation from Soviet invasion. His reputation as a Soviet puppet and oppressor of the Polish nation was confirmed by his post–martial law political actions in Poland. The West continued to support the Polish nation in its struggle against communism. An example of such support was the establishment of the Solidarity Foundation to support the union and other political opposition in Poland.

The dual-track U.S. policy toward Poland became more apparent when hostile relations with the authorities in Warsaw were no longer seen as a major obstacle to economic ties that would ease the hardship suffered by the Polish people under communist rule. Since there was no realistic alternative to the Polish military regime, a growing number of political organizations in the United States, among them the Polish American Congress, came out in favor of lifting economic sanctions and providing new credits for Warsaw. Decoupling political and economic relations, even if the communist authorities would derive direct political benefit from economic ties, emerged as the best way to address the complex situation. The Polish regime would continue to be isolated politically in the international arena, its illegitimate status emphasized at every occasion. Improving Poland's standard of living and preserving its international contacts would be implemented by economic means. In late 1985 Washington's policy toward Poland began to reflect a long-term strategy of responding to the urgent needs of the Polish people while preserving a tough and determined position on political issues.

United States–Polish relations at the beginning of 1986 resembled a war of nerves. The United States insisted that political changes should precede the lifting of economic sanctions, while Poland demanded the exact opposite of this sequence. In March 1986 the Reagan administration dispatched a retired ambassador for an unofficial visit to Poland, the Soviet Union, and West Germany—Walter J. Stoessel, Jr. The results of his meeting with General Jaruzelski were described as "frank and businesslike," implying a lack of agreement on major issues.[47]

The failure of the Stoessel mission provided the impetus for another round of the countries' propaganda duel. The Polish authorities issued a statement highly critical of the Reagan administration after the *Challenger* tragedy, and accused the United States of terrorism following the U.S. retaliatory strike against Libya. Commenting on the American astronauts who lost their lives in the *Challenger* disaster, the Polish *Żołnierz wolności* openly expressed its satisfaction: "These people were nevertheless participants in a program meant to permit the domination of space for the sake of a future victory during a confrontation on earth, a program in which the shuttles have been used as perfect tools for implementing the SDI plans—President Reagan's 'star wars.' "[48] Even the Soviet press would not lower itself to exploit this tragedy for political ends.

In response to the U.S. attack on Libya, Jerzy Urban, the government press spokesman in Warsaw, stated that this "barbaric" act was "a glaring example of arrogance and contempt for world opinion."[49] The United States was also accused of striving for military superiority over the Soviet Union, and of proclaiming the entire world as an area of vital interest for Washington. The conclusion was that Poland was one of several victims of the many U.S. shows of strength orchestrated by the Reagan administration.

Despite the inflammatory rhetoric, the Polish authorities surrendered to U.S. pressure on 22 July 1986, when a general amnesty was issued. The authorities unconditionally freed all political prisoners, including Zbigniew Bujak, a recently captured leader of the underground Solidarity who had defied the authorities for more than four years. Thus Poland met all three preconditions imposed by the United States for normalization: establishing a dialogue with the church; national reconciliation, supposedly achieved during the 1985 parliamentary elections; and the release of all political prisoners. The next step in improving U.S.-Polish relations had to be taken by Washington.

Washington's reaction to the amnesty was characteristically unenthusiastic, triggering criticism at home and abroad. The Reagan administration continued to refrain from any act that could be construed as endorsing Jaruzelski's regime. Numerous critics directed attention to some contradictory facts. First, even under the military dictatorship Poland was far more tolerant than neo-Stalinist Romania, for example. The Stalinist Romanian leadership, however, enjoyed the United States' most-favored-nation status as a reward for its independence from Moscow—despite the most flagrant human rights violations. Second, the U.S. disengagement from Poland served Soviet interests in Eastern Europe. According to one Western diplomat, Poland was sinking into "the Soviet morass."[50] Third, the pro-Soviet hard-liners in Warsaw, who constituted the main political challenge to Jaruzelski and his relatively moderate socioeconomic program, were strengthened by Washington's inability to appreciate political concessions that by Soviet standards were truly remarkable. Poland now had no political prisoners; it tolerated political opposition; it had an open-door policy regarding foreign travel; and the massive underground publication business had rendered government censorship ineffective. In fact, the Polish dictatorship was far less oppressive than some of the Third World regimes that were allies of the United States.

Polish public opinion was now unanimous in favor of lifting the economic sanctions. Seeing no better political alternative to Jaruzelski's regime, Lech Wałęsa and nine prominent Polish intellectuals issued a statement asking President Reagan to alter his hard-line approach to Poland, because socioeconomic deterioration threatened "the rulers and the ruled, those of us alive today as well as future generations." Moreover, the authors of this document concluded that further progress toward diversification in Poland would depend on "external stimuli," such as "the return of most-favored-nation status for Poland and access—on sensible, economically substantiated conditions—to U.S. government–guaranteed credits. In addition, Poland's programs would require the restoration and broadening of comprehensive scientific, cultural, and human contacts."[51]

This opposition statement was followed by two Polish-U.S. incidents. First, Poland in a propaganda exercise offered to provide the homeless in the United States with six thousand Polish blankets and sleeping bags in exchange for 50,000 tons of dry milk for Polish children after the Chernobyl accident. Second, in the summer of 1986 the Polish authorities publicized the defection of Colonel Ryszard Kukliński, an American informant on the Polish general staff. The Polish authorities stated that the U.S. government had been informed by Kukliński about the planned military crackdown in Poland in 1981, but had failed to warn Solidarity. Warsaw hoped to embarrass the Reagan administration, forcing it to explain why it withheld this information from the union, which on 13 December 1981 was caught by surprise. According to Warsaw, the Kukliński affair showed how unreliable the United States was an ally, and showed that the Reagan administration had merely used Solidarity as a tool against Moscow. The United States government ignored these allegations. In fact, warning Solidarity could have led to bloody civil strife if the union had chosen to challenge the military dictatorship. The U.S. attitude in this case was consistent with the policy of noninvolvement with any political group in Poland.

Another setback to U.S.–Polish relations was the Polish authorities' decision to deny an entry visa to U.S. senator Edward M. Kennedy, who in December 1986 planned to visit Poland and present two prominent leaders of Solidarity—Adam Michnik and Zbigniew Bujak—with the Robert F. Kennedy Human Rights Award. Senator Kennedy was also scheduled to talk with Lech Wałęsa, as well as with church and state officials. The Polish authorities, assuming that the meeting would be too provocative, in effect isolated Wałęsa and other top union leaders from official contacts with Western politicians; in October 1986 the Polish authorities had refused to grant a passport to Lech Wałęsa, who was to travel to the United States to receive a $10,000 prize from the John Rogers Foundation.

Polish government spokesman Jerzy Urban justified the refusal to allow Senator Kennedy to visit Poland by claiming that Polish public officials had an "overloaded schedule,"[52] but it was obviously a reaction to the United States' dual-track policy toward Poland. The message from Warsaw was that there is only one Poland—that represented by the communist authorities. Only Pope John Paul II was exempted from this rule; he was allowed to see both Jaruzelski and Wałęsa during his visit to Poland.

Even this hostile principle of Polish policy toward Western nations had to be modified if the remaining economic sanctions were to be lifted. When Deputy Secretary of State John C. Whitehead arrived in Warsaw in early 1987 for a fact-finding visit, his schedule included meetings with all three key players in Polish politics: General Jaruzelski, Lech Wałęsa, and Cardinal Glemp. His visit resulted in the restoration of most-favored-nation trading status for Poland and opened the way for an exchange of ambassadors.[53] The five-year diplomatic war between Washington and Warsaw was over.

General Jaruzelski's regime was satisfied that the United States had lifted all economic sanctions; but the balance sheet of U.S.-Polish relations for the first five years after the dismemberment of Solidarity was no cause for celebration. The nation had become polarized between its Soviet-sponsored rulers on one hand and the rest of the society on the other. General Jaruzelski conquered Poland and had to rule as a conqueror, however elaborate a facade his regime erected. All the socio-economic classes of Polish society were united to an unprecedented extent against the communist authorities. Unable to change the political order, the Polish people's apathy became one more economic sanction directed against the authorities. The combined effect of the U.S. and Polish economic sanctions against the communist regime was to paralyze the Polish economy. In less than a decade, Poland deteriorated from one of the top industrialized countries in the world to the level of a Third World state. Poland had become the economically backward and politically unstable ward of the Soviet Union. Preserving communism brought economic and moral destruction; but for General Jaruzelski it was a lesser evil.

The lifting of all U.S. sanctions formally ended over five years of tension between Washington and Warsaw and opened the way to an exchange of ambassadors between the two countries. Speaking on behalf of Solidarity, Lech Wałęsa concluded that "the decision taken by President Reagan is a consistent continuation of his policy of supporting the interests and aspirations of the Polish nation.[54] The official reaction in Warsaw to the lifting of the U.S. sanctions was positive but cautious. The Poles criticized the United States' "pragmatic sluggishness," but appreciated the change "from restrictions to realism."[55]

Normalizaton of relations, however, still had a long way to go. Poland had lost its share of the U.S. market, and the level of Polish trade with the United States, reduced to $255 million per year, would not increase rapidly. The authorities in Warsaw placed the entire blame for this historically unprecedented economic decline on the United States, knowing at the same time that the economic catastrophe was a by-product of the war conducted by the authorities against the Polish nation.

Political contacts between the two governments soon followed, with a visit to Washington by Józef Czyrek, the Central Committee secretary for international affairs, and then a visit by a six-member delegation of Polish parliamentarians. The Polish authorities made it clear that economic motives were the main driving force behind the opening with Washington. As Mr. Czyrek pointed out, his visit was aimed at "creating instruments that would enable us to obtain trade loans instead of paying cash for purchases: securing guaranteed loans . . . to promote such international fiscal mechanisms as the IMF, the World Bank, and the Paris Club."[56]

The United States continued its policy of dualism, that is, simultaneous contacts with the government and the opposition. Solidarity was awarded $1 million by the U.S. Congress to support social projects in Poland. Speaking for the union, Lech Wałęsa characterized U.S. aid as a "patriotic gesture"; the Polish government's spokesman described it as a "tip" for which "the heads of the former Solidarnosc have decided to commit political hara-kiri."[57]

Such political embarrassments did not stop Warsaw from seeking to improve diplomatic relations with Washington. When Vice-president George Bush decided to open his presidential campaign by making a highly publicized visit to Poland in October 1987, the authorities in Warsaw welcomed the opportunity to resume high-level contacts with the United States. The vice-president, however, met with representatives of all the main political forces in Poland, including the still outlawed union and the church; and he publicly advocated political pluralism.[58]

The solution to Poland's political problems was far from imminent, even after the sanctions had been lifted. The regime was still hopeful that meaningless steps like a referendum on the economic reforms proposed by the authorities would change the public perception of the communist regime and be acceptable as a substitute for legal recognition of the union. Consequently, U.S.-Polish relations were put on hold until the struggle for the political profile of Poland would be resolved. "The lack of any national accord at all," concluded U.S. deputy secretary of state John C. Whitehead, "produced a wait-and-see attitude in Washington and placed on hold domestic recovery in Poland."[59] Again, the country's future was dependent on whether the regime would reorganize the union representing the great majority of society.

The hesitant approach of the Polish authorities toward political reform delayed the return to business-as-usual relations between Poland and the United States for over two years. During 1987 and 1988 both sides adopted a wait-and-see attitude, awaiting domestic developments favorable to a reopening of broader political and economic relations. Deputy Secretary of State Whitehead's October 1988 visit to Poland reaffirmed the existence of a political stalemate between the two countries. Whitehead was quoted as saying that "the lack of any national accord" was the principal reason behind the American reluctance to offer new economic aid to Poland.[60] Premature resumption of economic relations between the two countries would suspend political evolution in Poland and would give the impression that the West could be satisfied with only minor adjustments in the way the communist authorities implemented their political monopoly of power.

The breakthrough in U.S.-Polish relations had to wait until July 1989, when President Bush arrived in Poland to back up the new accord between Solidarity leader Lech Wałęsa and the minister of internal affairs, Czesław Kiszczak. The visit was intended to demonstrate U.S. support for the emerging pluralism in Poland and to achieve reconciliation between the two nations and their governments. In this respect, the visit marked a turning point in bilateral relations and created the foundations for future cooperation.

It was agreed that both countries would work toward closer political consultations, economic cooperation, and scientific-technological exchange. In his address to the joint session of the Polish Sejm and the Senate, President Bush declared his intention to provide economic assistance to Poland in the form of a $100 million credit for development of the private sector of Polish economy, assignment of a $325 million credit from the World Bank for development of Polish agriculture and industry, a rescheduling of $940 million of the Polish debt to the United States that was due in 1989, and intervention on Poland's behalf to postpone the $5.2 billion repayment due in 1989 to other Western creditors.[61]

The U.S. plan to assist Poland on its road to political and economic recovery was a form of international ratification of the new social contract between Solidarity and the communist authorities. It opened a new stage in bilateral relations as well as in the international status of Eastern Europe as a whole. The United States was assuming responsibility for a peaceful transformation from communist totalitarianism and a command economy to democratic institutions and free enterprise. The United States was returning to the policy of peaceful engagement inside the Soviet sphere of influence and assuming an active role in the reconstruction of this region after four and a half decades of Soviet domination. The new pattern of U.S. relations with Poland began a major transformation of the political situation in Europe and the de-Stalinization of international relations among the East European states.

PART III

The Socialist State and the Union

CHAPTER FIVE

From Negotiations to a Military Solution

The birth of Solidarity, Poland's independent trade union, was both a domestic and an international event. For the Polish people it was an expression of hope for better economic conditions and increased participation in the political life of the country. In Washington and other Western capitals, the emergence of Solidarity was welcomed as a sure sign that the Soviet empire was disintegrating and that democratic aspirations among East European nations had persisted despite more than 30 years of Soviet domination. Moscow was alarmed, sensing a formidable challenge both to its strategic position in Europe and to the ideology that provided legitimacy for communist rule. Polish workers were in revolt against the state that claimed to represent and advance the interests of the workers. Equally threatening for the Soviet system of government was the fact that the revolt united over ten million workers of all social classes in a peaceful movement. The magnitude of this Polish revolt, unprecedented in history of all the East European uprisings against Soviet domination, hindered the use of military force to terminate the schism. Moscow knew that it was facing a united Polish nation likely to oppose the type of invasion that terminated previous revolts in Hungary and Czechoslovakia.

The initial policy of the Polish authorities toward the emerging trade union movement was to subordinate Solidarity to the political control of the communist party, allowing the union to negotiate only bread-and-butter issues. The key political question in the relations between Solidarity and the ruling communist party was the place this new organization would find in the structure of the socialist state. From the beginning of its negotiations with the striking workers, the government insisted that Solidarity respect the principle of party leadership; that is, the regime tried to subordinate the union to the direct control of the communist party and use it to renew confidence in the party. As they had done many times before, the communists searched for a formula that would allow them to ride an indigenous social movement and claim that they were an integral part of the working class.

After the Polish government became a party to the Gdańsk agreement with the union, the authorities adopted the policy that the party was an integral element of the changes demanded by the working class. The workers, according to the official view, wished to take matters into their own hands, because of the political leadership's past mistakes; but once all grievances were brought into the open, the party would consolidate its monopolistic leadership again.[1] The Gdańsk agreement was presented as the party's great success, a proof of its ability to recognize the distortions in socialist construction and reassert its supremacy in the nation's political life.

Special emphasis was placed on the proper understanding of the term "agreement." According to the party, this form of contract between the communist state and the workers had no bearing on the leading role of the party; it was not to be confused with a compromise that could imply a contractual limitation of communist power. The agreement was the party's public admission that a refurbishing of the socialist system was necessary, and an acknowledgment that the party was capable of carrying out the task of socialist renewal, while simultaneously opposing forces that could undermine the system's foundations. This double task, to absorb and adapt to change while preserving the supreme position of the party, was stated on many occasions, including the Central Committee's plenary session, when First Secretary Stanisław Kania explained:

> Our party is vitally interested in the development of social self-organization and social autonomy. This, of course, does not mean autonomy from the ideology and policy of socialism. It would mean an autonomous shaping of opinions and views on specific problems . . . Not only are social autonomy and the leading role of the party not contradictory, but they are mutually dependent . . .
>
> The party is the leading force of the nation. This position is expressed by the general lines of the historical process of socialist construction. It has been confirmed by the entire historical experience of People's Poland. The working class, the entire working population desire that the

party fulfill its leading role still better, that [the party] guarantee by its policy the fulfillment of their class interests, that [the party] create still better conditions for Poland's development.[2]

Any attempt to encroach on the exclusive political prerogatives of the party was immediately characterized as extremism and an attempt to create anarchy. The Gdańsk agreement was seen by the authorities as the culminating step of the spontaneous social movement. The next phase would be implemented unilaterally by the party. The key misunderstanding between the party and the union involved the issue of Poland's political process after the Gdańsk agreement. For Solidarity the agreement was only the beginning of a new political system that required continuous bargaining with the authorities. The party, however, perceived the agreement as a political solution that ended several weeks of crisis, allowing a return to the old communist "business as usual" model of politics. Apparently the communist leadership expected that the mere recognition of the workers' demands would disarm and fragment the union, leaving the party as Poland's sole political force. A similar strategy had defused mass demonstrations in October 1956. After the crisis was over, the authorities could slowly undo or twist the promises made under popular pressure.

Solidarity, however, succeeded in resisting the communists' demand that the leading role of the party should be incorporated into the union's statute. The Warsaw court that legalized the existence of an autonomous, independent, and self-governing trade union added an explicit reference to the supreme role of the communist party in all political activities. Eventually the Supreme Court allowed the union to drop this explicit reference on the grounds that it was a constitutional principle of universal application.

Solidarity's legalization implied that the new union approved the principles of the Polish socioeconomic system, including the leading role of the party and Poland's international alliances. Recognition of Solidarity did not imply that the party was ready to give up its ambition to be the decisive political force in Poland. The political transformation that was taking place in Poland was to be socialist in scope and nature.

The second point of the Gdańsk agreement stated:

In view of the establishment of new, independent and self-governing trade unions the Interfactory Strike Committee declares that they will observe the principles laid down in the Constitution of the Polish People's Republic. The new trade unions will defend the social and material interests of employees and do not intend to play the role of a political party. They approve of the principle that the means of production are social property—a principle that is the foundation of the socialist system in Poland. Recognizing that the PZPR plays the leading role in the state, and without undermining the actual system of international alliances, they seek to ensure for the working people suitable means of control, of expressing their opinions and of defending their rights.[3]

The actual statutes of the new union did not repeat this formula; it was argued that the agreement to abide by the constitution of the Polish state should satisfy the party's concern for the principles of the system. The Supreme Court, however, in granting legal status to the union, stipulated that it must recognize the leading role of the party in an unequivocal manner. Alliance to the party was included in a separate protocol. The union leadership decided to ignore this provision. "In our work," stated Lech Wałęsa, "we will be directed by our statutes as passed by us without the amendment, introduced by the court."[4]

Following the pattern established during the previous outbursts of discontent in 1956, 1970, and 1976, the communist authorities assumed that the "sausage approach" to the revolting workers would work again. When confronted with mass demonstrations and strikes, the authorities would defuse the situation by granting the workers a pay increase. In the 1970s Polish leader Edward Gierek introduced a program that included massive borrowing from the West to finance a higher standard of living and purchase political stability. After allowing the country to live on credit for several years, this program backfired. By the end of the decade, Poland had accumulated about $20 billion in foreign debt and had no resources to pay it back. The regime lost credibility as the symptoms of economic catastrophe affected every household. The Poles revolted and eventually gained the right to establish a free and independent union, limits on censorship, the right to strike, and a substantial pay increase. This economic concession was no longer feasible, however, because the regime had no resources to underwrite a higher standard of living. Pay raises of up to 20 percent, combined with declining productivity, fueled inflation and spiraling demands and strikes.

The ongoing struggle between the newly formed union and the authorities generated internal instability, which was seen as a threat to the security of the state, as well as to the social and economic order. Solidarity's appearance was also an international issue; it threatened the security of the Soviet leadership in Moscow. Poland occupied a central place in Soviet strategy; and the Kremlin's fears of any ruling communist party's losing its hold on its nation were known to be enough to provoke a military response. The task of controlling militant groups within the union and the party became one of the central tasks of both organizations—and the key to survival.

The authorities hoped that the official recognition of Solidarity would alienate the union leadership from the rank-and-file workers. As members of the establishment, the union leadership was eventually expected to side with the authorities, thus becoming another link in the transmission belt between the party and the working class. An alternative development, the transformation of the union into a political party, would be regarded as a violation of the Gdańsk agreement and a threat to national security. The Soviet Union was not prepared to tolerate a state of dyarchy, that is, the existence of two opposing centers of power in Poland.

The threat to the Soviet-type system in Poland came from several directions. In addition to the economic crisis that affected the entire society's living standard and Poland's contribution to the Warsaw Pact's defense, the social movement in Poland rekindled the debate about the legitimacy of the communist system. A group of Polish intellectuals associated with the Committee for the Defense of Workers (Polish acronym, KOR) confronted the party with four political accusations.

The KOR pointed out, first, that the existing system of government had no grass-roots support; it was imposed by the Soviets after their victory over Nazi Germany. Second, Poland's economic and political ties with the Soviet Union were the leading cause of the persistent crisis in Poland. Only a pro-Western orientation of the Polish state could bring prosperity and stability. Third, the Polish nation could never be governed in a totalitarian fashion. As long as Western-style social democracy was banned from Poland, the country would continue to experience chronic socioeconomic problems. Fourth, communism had produced an enormous social cleavage in Poland. The ruling elite monopolized political and economic power and was using its privileged position to oppress and exploit the great majority of the society.

Since the KOR was instrumental in shaping Solidarity's political platform, the Polish authorities feared an eventual radicalization of the union. If it became a political party, Solidarity would be compelled to challenge the communist government in Poland, and thereby jeopardize the nation's security. It was taken for granted in Warsaw that Moscow would not allow an independent, noncommunist Poland to exist. From the beginning of the 1980 crisis, the Polish authorities were very sensitive to the influence of the so-called extremists, who appeared to be willing to gamble Poland's independence for a chance to change the sociopolitical system. In this context, the introduction of martial law was seen as a necessary step to protect the nation from the catastrophic consequences that would arise from the plans of the political opposition—rather than as a defense of the communist party's monopoly of power.

The leaders of the opposition were optimistic, however, that far-reaching political changes could be implemented, and that the Soviets could be deterred from invading the country. Jacek Kuroń, one of the key activists of the Committee for the Defense of Workers, calculated that "the Polish people can organize themselves in such a way that the Soviets would not take such a step. That can happen only in the moment of explosion. And then it would not be a new Prague, but a situation like the one in Afghanistan. If I may make the comparison, it might possibly be a second Budapest, as in 1956. But we will do everything to prevent it."[5]

It is surprising that Solidarity's leaders had never devoted serious attention to the issue of Poland's place in the European balance of power, and particularly to Poland's relations with the Soviet Union. Preoccupied with internal Polish affairs, the union failed to take into account the influence Moscow had on the communist authorities in Poland, or the Soviet determination to preserve the status quo in Eastern Europe. The popularity of the union, the membership of which exceeded the party's ranks by four to one within less than six months, created the strong impression of great power based on genuine public support. The union became oblivious to the fact that public support in communist societies has always come second after the ability to project raw physical power.

This mistake by Solidarity's leaders can also be explained by looking at the internal dynamics of the movement. This truly democratic and procedure-oriented organization paid relatively little attention to long-term goals and grand objectives. In its optimistic perception of reality, the union became accustomed to solving problems as they arose, without paying too much attention to more distant obstacles. A Soviet military invasion or a military crackdown executed by the Polish security forces, was unthinkable; and for this reason no preventive steps were taken to prepare for such possibilities. Solidarity did not share the communist assumption that a direct relationship existed between Poland's socialism and Poland's independence. The union did not see itself as threatening to Moscow since its ambitions were confined to the borders of the Polish state. Its extensive contacts with the West, and the enthusiastic support it received there, were considered natural and of no consequence to the security of Poland or its neighbors. Thus Solidarity underestimated both the communist determination to stay in power regardless of the immediate socioeconomic consequences and the potential long-term effects of its activities on the Soviet system of government.

Another major mistake committed by Solidarity was the excessive use of strikes as political weapons. Owing to the authorities' reluctance to yield ground, the threat of a strike accompanied every single demand put forward by the union. Eventually the authorities could with some degree of success charge Solidarity with the responsibility for deepening the economic crisis and sparking political anarchy. Strikes were a very frequent phenomenon in Poland during the legal existence of Solidarity, and occasionally strikes were organized for trifling reasons or for no reason at all—and frequently despite the opposition of the church. The union's decentralized structure created the impression of atomization and diversity, which could undermine the unity of the entire society. Solidarity devoted too much time and energy to organizational and procedural matters, and to negotiations among its members and with the authorities, instead of developing a workable program of economic and social reforms that would put the authorities on the defensive.

In addition to the threat from Solidarity, the security of Poland was in danger owing to major changes in the ranks of the Polish communist party. The second most important development in Poland during the legal existence of Solidarity was the ninth congress of the Polish communist party in mid-July 1981. A party congress usually takes place only once every five years. However, the eighth congress, in February 1980, had been dominated by Edward Gierek, the party's first secretary at that time, and his loyalists; it had failed to address the economic and social crisis. Consequently, after the removal of the party leadership responsible for the crisis following the emergence of Solidarity, and in response to the pressure from rank-and-file party members, the new leadership agreed to call an extraordinary meeting of the party.

Preparation for the ninth congress began in the fall of 1980. Three distinct groups within the party clashed openly during the lengthy preparations. The first group was made up of the rank-and-file members who insisted on an honest assessment of the mistakes that had caused the crisis, as well as a major overhaul of the internal party structure to prevent similar mistakes, and the personalization of political power, in the future. This group succeeded in democratizing the practice for selecting delegates and won the right to secret balloting during the congress. The democratic revolution that affected the working class in Poland also affected the communist party itself; the electoral slogan of the young party radicals called for a "crossing out of the party apparatus" to open the door for new activists. In effect, the iron rule of the Leninist party—the principle of democratic centralism—was violated, and it was expected that the congress would turn into a spontaneous, runaway affair unprecedented in the history of the party. The freedom to criticize communist policies could greatly damage the Polish authorities as well as their patrons in Moscow, who on numerous occasions protested and threatened the Polish leadership with serious consequences, including invasion, should the trend toward democracy be left unchecked.

A similar democratic congress scheduled by the Czechoslovakian communist party in 1968 was the immediate cause for deploying the Soviet troops against Prague. Since the Polish people, even the communists, were not allowed to exercise freedom under the existing order in Eastern Europe, the main task of the ruling group within the party was to contain the democratic trends. As First Secretary Stanisław Kania observed, unless the leadership were in a position to dominate the meeting, "there wouldn't be any congress."[6] The choices left to the party officials were either to restrain the liberal rebellion within the party or to face a Soviet invasion.

The second group within the Polish communist party was the party's ruling center. This group was confronted not only with a powerful liberal wing, but also with a numerically insignificant, but politically threatening, conservative group called the Katowice Forum—the third competing group. The Katowice Forum charged the Polish hierarchy with "revisionism and opportunism." The historical roots of neo-Stalinism in Poland date back to the immediate post–World War II era, when a group of ultraorthodox communists was sent from Moscow to take over political power and watch after Soviet interests. These so-called Muscovites had never been entirely purged from the ranks of the Polish party, and now the second generation of hard-liners saw an opportunity for a political comeback. Anticipating a Soviet invasion similar to those in Hungary and Czechoslovakia, the conservatives pressed for a "knockout" solution for the unruly Solidarity and a return to the disciplined and centralized form of communist order as practiced under Stalin and in some East European satellites, notably Husák's Czechoslovakia.

The political program advocated by the hard-liners was economically unrealistic, and it was provocative and insulting to Polish national aspirations. The difficulty in dealing with this fraction was the confidence they enjoyed in Moscow, especially during Brezhnev's tenure in the Kremlin. They offered the ever-suspicious Soviet leadership a tempting alternative to the centrists, who advocated moderate reforms and might be persuaded by the prevailing liberal mood to overstep the limits of Soviet tolerance. The hard-liners were seen by Moscow as a valuable political asset in Poland's domestic scene, a constant reminder of the Stalinist alternative, and a counterweight to liberal tendencies within the party. At the time of Solidarity's emergence, they weakened the ruling group and restricted their freedom of political maneuver. The centrists were struggling on both sides of the political spectrum, and the uncertainties surrounding the extraordinary party congress were magnified into overt factionalism.

The economic reforms advanced by the moderates within the communist party envisioned no political changes beyond a few adjustments in the facade of popular support, primarily in granting local authorities more decision-making authority in matters not essential to the political system. In the economic life of the nation, the reforms put forward an inherently contradictory program: to strengthen central planning while expanding self-management at the enterprise level. The main thrust of the proposed changes was to overcome bureaucratic inertia and the passive attitudes of the workers by forcing enterprises to operate according to the principles of profitability—without diminishing the authorities' ability to manage the national economy according to their own priorities. The proposed reforms would result in a considerable democratization of Poland's economic and political life, but would not alter the structure of the communist state. In sum, the government's program envisioned an overhaul of the decision-making procedure regarding the national economy—without any changes in politics.

The centrists who followed Kania's and, after October 1981, General Jaruzelski's leadership prevailed at the congress and retained the dominant position in the party. Their political victory was of dubious value, however, since the extraordinary congress produced no extraordinary changes in the membership of the ruling elite or in the political program of the party. The results of the congress were disappointing. There were no changes for the national economy; nor were any pluralistic tendencies approved. "The delegates," noted an observer of Polish politics, "appeared preoccupied with settling old scores, apportioning blame for the crisis and voting out of office anyone tainted by the mistakes of the previous leadership. Remarkably little attention was paid to the future and the meeting failed to agree on a vision and a program for getting out of the crisis."[7] The only positive outcome of the extraordinary congress was that it vented a lot of popular passion while managing not to incite Moscow further.

With its power consolidated, the centrist leadership was free to apply a Stalinist knockout solution to the crisis and endorse limited economic reforms that offered some hope for a better future. With the reinforcement of the status quo came socioeconomic immobilization, a national paralysis that on one hand frustrated the political aspirations of the Poles and on the other hand created a public inertia that neutralized the communists' ability to rule, or even to implement minor economic reforms.

Poland remained loyal to the Soviets within the Warsaw Pact and the CMEA, and the party returned to its sacred democratic centralism after defeating the idea of "horizontal structures," which it was hoped would permit direct communication between the lower echelons of the party organization without obtaining clearance from the central authorities in Warsaw.[8]

Since the congress offered no solution to the economic crisis and made no changes to accommodate Solidarity politically, some breakthrough other than political accommodation was required; this state of affairs was understood by both sides. The union's metamorphosis into a political party was accelerated in the second half of 1981, culminating in a call for free elections—which without any doubt would remove the communist party from any political role in Poland. At the same time the party halted its retreat under the continuing pressure of Solidarity by proclaiming that its potential for additional compromise had been exhausted, and it demanded a moratorium on strikes. The polarization of political attitudes that followed the extraordinary congress was a prelude to martial law, which put an end to sixteen months of liberty and democracy in Poland.

The tone of official statements regarding Solidarity hardened appreciably in the few months preceding the implementation of martial law. Renewed emphasis on the leading role of the communist party as the anchor of Polish internal order and sovereignty testified to the offensive posture of the authorities. The party's perception of Solidarity had changed considerably, from a legitimate expression of anger by the working class to a conspiracy by a group of political adventurers against the party, the working class, and the socialist state. Political rights in Poland were to be limited to the communist party and two other groups that acted jointly with the communists. The existence of Solidarity was declared to be the reason for the internal difficulties, the external threat, and the barrier to economic reforms. A statement issued by the secretariat of the Polish communist party reaffirmed the authorities' new assertiveness. It stated, among other things, that

> No one should count on the fact that he may succeed in separating the party from the work force, that the plant organization and their leadership will succumb to pressure and threats. Behind our party there stands unquestioned historical achievement and the fact that it has been—and is now, with the working class—proceeding along a path of profound transformations, reforms and accords, approved by the nation ... The PZPR, faithful to the ideas of Marxism-Leninism and to its class tradition, treats as its supreme objective and its main duty patriotic service to the nation, and concern for the interests of working people.[9]

The party had regained its poise and was ready to fight back.

Several events proceeded the introduction of martial law. In October General Jaruzelski had been elected first secretary, thereby adding the top party position to the top position in the government and armed forces. Next, military teams were dispatched to inspect local authorities and economic enterprises, and report violations of the law. This was a dress rehearsal for martial law, which gave the authorities the opportunity to develop a list of individuals to be interned. Finally, the Politburo requested that the government enact legislation suspending the right to strike. Since strikes were the union's only weapon for opposing the authorities, this step must be regarded as highly provocative and an attempt to induce Solidarity to make a political move that would give the authorities a casus belli.

The imposition of martial law on the night of 12 December 1981 was seen as necessary for two reasons. First, a military confrontation with the nation—represented by Solidarity—was presented as the only way left to break the domestic stalemate. The government declared that the platform of partnership with the union was dissolved once Solidarity entered a fight for power that would undermine the communist character of the Polish state. Martial law was imperative, in the authorities' view, because the fate of both the Polish state and the Polish nation was at stake, since continuing the confrontation with the union would result in civil war. Martial law was, in the words of General Jaruzelski, "a lesser evil than the fratricidal conflict which not so long ago stood at our threshold." His conclusion was that Solidarity should bear total responsibility for both the crisis and the way it was to be resolved.[10]

The Italian newspaper *La Stampa* had the following comment on Jaruzelski's theory of the lesser evil:

> However, no one defines for us the greater evil that Poland would have experienced . . . If one wants to guess, the first hypothesis that logically comes to mind is that of Soviet intervention.
>
> Except that this hypothesis is firmly denied and contested by both Moscow and Warsaw. Almost offended, they maintain that the USSR never intended to intervene in Poland and that both the choice and the action were an internal Polish matter. But in that case, there still is no explanation of what the greater evil would be from which Jaruzelski supposedly has saved the country by imposing the lesser evil. Perhaps one might think of a possible civil war, concealed in the message of the general. In fact, in the first days there was an attempt at presenting the Solidarnosc labor union centers as dens of an armed revolt in the making. That fabricated story was soon dispelled when the demonstrators, including those who were occupying the mines, did not display weapons

and the militarized television was able to show on the TV screen only five pistols found in the labor union centers—near a heap of books and leaflets. The only weapon with which Solidarnosc could counter the armed forces was free speech.[11]

The second reason given for imposing martial law was related to the situation in Europe. As the deputy prime minister of Poland, Mieczysław Rakowski, succinctly phrased it, "We rescued Poland and Europe."[12] Without making it more explicit, this relatively liberal member of General Jaruzelski's ruling team implied that the civil strife in Poland could have escalated into a regional conflict involving all of Eastern Europe, because Moscow and its satellites would not sit idly and observe the triumph of Polish nationalism over the system imposed by the Soviet regime. Unlike the confrontations in Hungary and Czechoslovakia, a Polish-Soviet confrontation could escalate into armed conflict between Warsaw Pact and NATO forces. This logic led Rakowski to the conclusion that the West European states should be grateful to the Polish military authorities for saving Europe from military conflict. Instead of condemning the suppression of Solidarity, the West should help General Jaruzelski by offering him substantial means to buy support for his policies. The military dictatorship in Warsaw expected the democratic states of the West to approve and underwrite the military takeover of Poland.

The military solution of the Polish crisis was a historical tragedy for the Polish people, their hopes for a better life, and their democratic aspirations. The real villain of this ugly episode was Moscow, which pushed its puppets in Warsaw to subdue the Polish nation while claiming to have no part in the affair. Another experiment with democracy ended in a serious setback; the unarmed Polish people were unable to extract the most basic rights from the communist dictatorship. An attempt to work out a political partnership with the ruling communist party, which was guilty of an unprecedented mismanagement of the social and economic life of the nation, had been brutally rejected after a period of political maneuvering and negotiations designed to buy time for the regime.

The hypocrisy of Soviet-style communism, which claimed to represent the interests and aspirations of working people, was demonstrated once more in Poland, as it had been in Hungary and Czechoslovakia, where similar attempts to add self-management and a human face to the Soviet system were destroyed. The military action against Solidarity, that is, against the entire Polish nation, provided further evidence of communism's inability to reform and move beyond its selfish and narrow-minded political interest. The incompetence of the communist authorities' social and economic policies were well documented during the brief legal existence of Solidarity before martial law was imposed. Their inability to build a stable political system supported by genuine public consensus was demonstrated by their resort to martial law.

The Polish coup indicated that the armed forces of the Soviet satellites were commanded and controlled by the Soviet generals and marshals, and could be used to pacify their own nation. As in so many other crises since the Bolshevik victory in Russia, the imperial ambitions of Moscow took priority over the rights of smaller nations and the ideals of socialism, which the Soviets profess. Once more, the Russians prevailed while the cause of socialism lost.

Most communist parties in the West condemned this Soviet invasion executed by Moscow's proxies in Warsaw, and expressed solidarity with the victims of the Soviet policy. Only the French communists sided with Jaruzelski and Moscow; they quickly received recognition for their "understanding of the difficult situation in which [Poland] has found itself." In a letter to Georges Marchais, the secretary general of the French communist party, General Jaruzelski proceeded to thank "dear Comrade Marchais" for "confirmation of the international solidarity of the great movement to which our two parties belong."[13] One is free to conclude that the great movement General Jaruzelski was referring to had as its principal objectives the subjugation of Polish national aspirations and a brutal domineering over the working people.

After martial law was imposed in Poland the political fortunes of communist parties in Western Europe began to decline, signaling the decline of communism as an ideology and a political power in the industrialized states. The Polish workers who organized Solidarity delivered a historic blow to Marxism-Leninism in Poland and the rest of Europe. The declaration of martial law, which included the arrest of thousands of Solidarity leaders and police attacks on factories, confirmed the anti-humanitarian essence of communism.

Chapter Six

The Politics of Self-Destruction

Unlike János Kádár after 1956 and Gustáv Husák after 1968, General Jaruzelski in 1982 had no quick palliative to bring about economic well-being and political compliance. The internal invasion that destroyed the organizational structure of Solidarity was a temporary political solution; it complicated rather than facilitated the task of solving the economic crisis, which required slow and painful economic reforms. Besides a far-reaching economic restructuring, Poland desperately needed Western credits to subsidize and finance economic programs, and easy access to Western technological know-how to modernize its technological base.

This simple reality placed General Jaruzelski in an uncomfortable position: the more he played Moscow's political game in Poland, the more he depended on Western economic assistance. After the internationalization of the Polish economy in the 1970s, Poland's dependence on the West became a permanent feature of internal politics. The key dilemma that confronted Jaruzelski's regime immediately after the declaration of martial law was how to freeze the political aspirations of the population and at the same time stimulate economic renewal, which required social dynamism and the West's active involvement. The zeal for erasing Solidarity from the pages of Polish history was matched only by the pressure to elaborate a new, more rational economic system that remained within the political canons of a communist state.

General Jaruzelski's calculations for solving the Polish crisis were rooted in the assumption that, in his words, "Solidarity is a dying phenomenon . . . The society—that is, the majority—is identified neither with the government nor with the opposition. The center supports neither side. It wants peace, work, reform, normalization. And the government offers that guarantee." The general concluded that through the aggressive promotion of economic reforms, emotional attachment to the union would fade away and prosperity would divert attention from political ambitions.[1] It is surprising how ignorant this self-proclaimed Marxist-Leninist was of the organic relations between politics and economics, and of the capacity of the opposition to resist the authorities. The underground Solidarity developed a strategy of "frontal refusal," which called for "ignoring all actions of the authorities, with the exception, of course, of ones directly affecting us, such as those by the police, which have to be counteracted, and organizing various forms of independent activities in science, education, and culture, outside the influence of the authorities."[2]

Having imprisoned the opposition, General Jaruzelski consolidated his position within the party leadership and began to rebuild the social roots of the party. At the seventh Central Committee plenum in February 1982, the first plenum after the declaration of martial law, General Jaruzelski prevailed over the neo-Stalinist hard-liners and strengthened his authority before leaving for consultations in Moscow. He committed the party to reforms, stating that

> Martial law is not a goal in itself . . . It does not mean the reforms are being frozen. We are confirming that in our action. It is only in the essential calm conditions that the planned reforms can be implemented and laws introduced which are the foundation of the development and consolidation of socialist democracy. Despite all the difficulties we are determined to continue along this path. The line of socialist renewal cannot be abandoned, nor can there be any regression.[3]

The general failed to realize that although he could speak for the party, his capacity to mobilize the society was reduced to nothing. Solidarity's aim was to achieve freedom from communist totalitarianism. When the compromise between society and the government was rejected by imposing martial law, society responded with resignation and apathy. This social mood became the single biggest foe of the post–martial law communist regime. The first evidence of this new attitude became apparent in February 1982, when the authorities increased the prices of food and energy by up to 400 percent without provoking social opposition. A few months before, such a step would have triggered a general strike and nationwide demonstrations. Now, the public did not care—an attitude that helped Jaruzelski subdue the nation, but otherwise made his rule ineffective.

The crisis of confidence was not the only cause of Jaruzelski's vulnerability. His actions eliminated Solidarity, but left intact the party, the principal cause of political instability in the country. In consequence, the claim that martial law was a necessary step to save the nation did not appear very credible. The practical outcome of this action was the preservation of the party and the despised communist system, which even by official accounts is responsible for 20 years of crisis during its 40-year administration. Convincing arguments against communism in Poland were put forward by Adam Schaff, one of the founders of the modern communist party, who in the late 1950s and the 1960s had been regarded as the chief ideologue in Warsaw. His "original sin" theory on the origins of communism in Poland was elaborated in a book entitled *The Communist Movement at a Crossroads* (Vienna, 1982), in which he accused Moscow and the Soviet men in Poland, who from 1945 carried out the decision to impose communism, of creating "bureaucratic socialism" and the "dictatorship of the apparatus" instead of democratic socialism and the dictatorship of the proletariat.

This conquest theory of Polish communism led Schaff to the conclusion that the party has never gained legitimacy and was never able to govern except when its policies were endorsed by the popular and powerful Catholic church. The military takeover in Poland created the conditions for correcting this original mistake, in view of the enormous popularity and prestige enjoyed by the armed forces among the Polish people. General Jaruzelski, however, made a historic mistake somewhat similar to the mistake committed by Władysław Gomułka, who after the successful revolt of October 1956 left the Stalinist wing of the party intact and permitted the party apparatus to survive and subsequently re-emerge as the center of power.

Jaruzelski's preservation of the communist bureaucracy guaranteed the continuity of the old, discredited communist order and frustrated the implementation of reforms. Neo-Stalinists at the top diluted the reform program, and the lower-level functionaries blocked implementation of the enacted legislation. It was soon apparent that martial law had brought back the old system and many old faces; no solution to either the political or the economic problems was forthcoming. As a result, Jaruzelski's regime combined physical strength and political weakness. He began to rule by force, and was never able to attract a popular consensus.

An official commitment to reforming the national economy was supplemented by the pledge to solve political problems through a dialogue with the nation. The first step in Jaruzelski's policy of "dialogue" was the internment of the Solidarity leadership; this was soon followed by the delegalization of the union. Relations with the church were not terminated, however. Despite severe strains, meetings between Cardinal Glemp and General Jaruzelski were scheduled over two to three months. Cardinal Glemp's soft policy toward the regime—his de facto acceptance of the need for introducing martial law—facilitated state-church relations, but produced deep divisions among the Polish clergy, which favored a more determined stand against communism. Having rejected the idea of dialogue with Solidarity, even under the condition that it would operate as a trade union and not as a political organization, the regime moved to build a new political facade of dialogue with a political institution that could be controlled from the inside. Within the first year of military rule in Poland, it became clear that, like his predecessors, Jaruzelski had no intention of permitting political pluralism and legalizing the political opposition. His obsession with discipline and order, and his preference for loyalty rather than competence, hindered an imaginative and open-minded approach to the gigantic problems confronting his nation.

The first months of martial law were a time of internal party consolidation through purges. The party lost more than 800,000 members (or over 30 percent),[4] but those who decided to stay were more reliable. The party's next task called for displacing the armed forces as the key pillar of the system. The transfer of power back to the party was not completed until about two years later, but the party was recovering from its political defeat under strong Soviet pressure to return to civilian rule.

Once the party regained its ability to rule, the construction of a new political facade progressed. Solidarity was officially dissolved on 8 October 1982 and replaced by a new union that also claimed to be independent and self-managed, but in reality was dominated by the party. In disbanding Solidarity, General Jaruzelski broke his promise to restore Solidarity as a union, indicating that his idea of a dialogue was only a one-way street. The pattern of future political solutions in Poland was set. If a social organization refused to submit, it would be dissolved and replaced by a more cooperative substitute. One year after the ban on Solidarity, the authorities liquidated the independent organization of Polish writers and set up the Union of Polish Writers, which was subordinated to the party. This new organization immediately adopted an ideological-programmatic declaration, formulated by the party, accepting Poland's existing political system.[5] Such was the nature of Jaruzelski's normalization.

At the end of 1982, the regime suspended some of the provisions of martial law to initiate a gradual, step-by-step process that would culminate in the lifting of the state of war on 22 July 1983. Parallel to this apparent normalization was the incorporation of all the key provisions of martial law into civil law. The new legislation forbade a worker to leave his job without permission from management. The new trade union's right to strike could be exercised only after all lengthy and complex legal procedures had been exhausted. Participation in an unauthorized strike was sufficient cause to fire an employee. A new constitutional amendment granted the State Council, Poland's collective executive, the authority to "introduce martial law in part of the Polish People's Republic or in the whole if considerations of defense or an external threat to the security of the state so require. For the same reason, the State Council may declare partial or general mobilization."[6] In this way the regime acquired constitutional bases for reintroducing martial law. Before this amendment was enacted, the Polish constitution provided for the declaration of a "state of war" only in case of a threat to national security.

Another piece of legislation, entitled "Special Legal Regulations during the Period of Overcoming the Socioeconomic Crisis and Changes in Some Laws," gave the management of enterprises—defined as "fundamental . . . for the national economy or for the state's defense," public service enterprises, and "enterprises that meet the needs of the population"—discretionary power to dissolve any organization unwilling to cooperate with the authorities.[7] Finally, the Soviet-style "social parasite" law made working mandatory, and economic enterprises were obligated to provide employment for "certain categories of people directed to take up jobs under compulsory recruitment" and those "who shirk work."[8] This new labor code was compared by the church to the "feudal binding of the farmer to the land."[9]

In August 1983 a new law concerning the control of publications and public enterprises was introduced. Its recognition of freedom of speech as one of the fundamental constitutional principles was followed by a statement that proclaimed state interests supreme. Article 2, Point 1, of the old legislation provided that "while availing oneself of freedom of speech, printed matter, and public performance, one must not attack the independence or territorial integrity of the PZPR." The new censorship law added, "or threaten the state's security." In addition, Point 5 of Article 2, which stated that one must not "disclose anything that constitutes a state secret, an economic secret, or an official secret concerning defense and the armed forces," was supplemented with the phrase, "or in any other way endanger state defense."[10] Clearly, the authorities intentionally created vague and sweeping legislation to create an enormous, arbitrary power of censorship and control over the intellectual life of the nation.

In practice, the draconian censorship law had very little impact, owing to the enormous underground publishing business operating in Poland. It is estimated that more than 1,000 bulletins, several monthly and quarterly magazines, and at least 50 books were published in Poland annually by illegal printing houses. The largest of these—NOVA—claimed to issue 30 titles, or 150,000 volumes, in just nine months.[11] It became a financially independent corporation, capable of paying royalties to its authors and salaries to its employees, and supported the families of detained activists. The censorship law was ineffective, too, because Polish citizens had extensive contacts with families and friends in the West, and easy access to information provided by Radio Free Europe, Voice of America, and numerous other Western radio stations.

The regime probably had little hope of achieving public indoctrination or acceptance of the system. Its rule was rooted in its ability to apply terror at any time and place; this seemed to satisfy Jaruzelski's political aspirations. He displayed no ambition to become a popular and charismatic leader enthusiastically supported by the masses. The public's understanding that he was powerful enough to terrorize the entire nation if necessary was the cornerstone of consensus in his Poland.

The Jaruzelski government's attempt to put new makeup on the old face of the totalitarian state was exemplified by the establishment of the Patriotic Movement of National Rebirth (Polish acronym, PRON). This theoretically independent and self-governing political organization was set up to encourage people of various political orientations to work together for the welfare of the nation. Its philosophical base was supposed to be a humanitarianism that would unite Marxists and Christians in a broad social movement motivated by patriotism. In 1983 PRON was granted the constitutional status that the party had denied to the Catholic church, which represents at least 80 percent of the Polish population. The constitutional amendment described PRON as "a platform of unity for the nation's patriotic forces . . . and also a platform of joint activity by the political parties, social organizations and associations, and citizens, regardless of their outlook, on matters concerning the functioning of the socialist state and the country's comprehensive development." However, to discourage any misunderstanding concerning the procommunist character of PRON, the constitutional amendment also stated that "the alliance and cooperation of the PZPR with ZSL [United Peasant Party] and SD [Democratic Party] in the building of socialism, and their joint activity with the social organizations and associations that support the political principals of the PZPR, forms the basis of the Patriotic Movement for National Rebirth (PRON)."[12] In other words, PRON was General Jaruzelski's version of the old united front formula, in which communists dominated and hid behind a front organization claiming broad popular support for some vague and noncontroversial cause.

The immediate political objective of PRON was to invite the church, or at least some individual clergy, to collaborate with the authorities, and to create an impression of socialist pluralism in the political life of the country. Jan Dobraczynski, a popular Catholic writer, was named chairman of the PRON's national council; however, the national council's daily affairs were directed by Marian Orzechowski, a Soviet-educated member of the communist party secretariat and foreign minister, who was well known as a political hard-liner. According to the available data only 32 percent of PRON's members belonged to the communist party; however, a further 20 percent were members of the two other legal parties associated with the communists, which in practice gave the regime enough influence to monopolize this organization. The remaining 48 percent of PRON's members claimed no political affiliation.

Such was the nature of General Jaruzelski's dialogue with the opposition and his search for national reconciliation. In reality, the regime rejected any form of dialogue with the Polish people and continued to impose its own organizational and political solutions. There were no negotiations between the state on one hand and the church and the free union on the other about developing a national platform for dealing with the progressing crisis that would be acceptable to all parties, including the Soviets. Communism's classical arrogance of power and unyielding attitude prevailed in Warsaw. Cardinal Glemp called Jaruzelski's approach to the nation "a false dialogue when one side says it will not concede one inch."[13]

The great gap between the rulers and the ruled remained unbridged. The majority of society escaped into "internal immigration," that is, private social, economic, or cultural activities away from the state's interference. The Polish people revenged the loss of Solidarity and their hopes for freedom and welfare by a passive unwillingness to work.

The military regime's human rights record was not the worst in the Soviet bloc, but numerous basic rights were violated. Approximately six thousand Solidarity activists were arrested in the initial stage of martial law, and about twenty people were killed during the police invasions of enterprises occupied by protesting workers. By the end of 1982, the authorities began to release interned unionists, except the better-known individuals. The first general amnesty was declared on 22 July 1983. The regime's policy was to avoid the international embarrassment that could result from detaining large numbers of political prisoners, by categorizing most of the politically motivated offenses as common criminal cases.

These cases included the collection of money in support of imprisoned activists and their families, distribution of illegal publications, and similar acts of defiance against the state. The redefinition of political offenses not only reduced the number of political prisoners admitted by the regime; it also allowed the government to extend the provisions of the Amnesty Act to political inmates without creating an impression of weakness. Thus under the 1983 Amnesty Act more than 8,500 individuals were released, and an unspecified number of people who had been hiding underground revealed themselves to the authorities and were released under the amnesty law.[14]

State-generated propaganda linked the underground Solidarity with reports of unsuccessful attempts to bomb hospitals, schools, and other public places, and illegal possession of arms. In almost every case the profile of the people involved included illegal printing activities or travels to the West, allegedly for terrorist training. The obvious purpose was to equate the underground union with terrorism, link it to the Western intelligence centers, and deter people from supporting the union. Association with the union implied participation in activities that endangered vital national security interests. Underground Solidarity was presented to the Polish people not as a union of Polish workers, but as a foreign agency engaged in political subversion.

Facing international scrutiny of its internal politics, Jaruzelski's government preferred to intimidate and impose economic sanctions against politically insubordinate individuals, rather than keep them in jail. The policy of repression orchestrated by the regime reflected external pressures applied by both Moscow and the West. Responding to the Soviet demand for toughness, the regime treated demonstrators brutally and arrested many. Then, to placate the West, it quickly released the jailed arrestees, claiming that normalization had been accomplished. A cyclical pattern of arrests, releases, and rearrests was repeated several times until the 1986 amnesty, which was prompted by a desire to remove the U.S. economic sanctions.

Management of physical power was the only political mechanism available to the regime. The authorities had sticks, but no carrots; even the most naive members of Polish society could not believe a better future would result from another price increase. Beating its citizens to submission and directing their attention to private economic affairs were the regime's methods of coping with resistance. The Polish internal security forces acquired a degree of power that even the top leadership occasionally found difficult to control and politically embarrassing. By June 1984 there were 72 documented cases of Solidarity activists being murdered in mysterious circumstances; the police were unable to find the perpetrators.

Very little effort was made to conceal police involvement in these crimes, since official investigations were either never initiated or dropped without any attempt to search for the assailants. The victims included workers and students engaged in antigovernment activities.[15]

The best-known victim of police homicide during the early stages of martial law was Grzegorz Przemyk, a high school student arrested by the police during street demonstrations in Warsaw. After he was beaten by the security forces and denied medical assistance for two days, he died on the operating table. A public outcry about police lawlessness and strong international condemnation impelled the authorities to charge the doctors with failing to provide medical care and to charge two ambulance drivers with indirectly causing the boy's death. Only the ambulance drivers were sentenced, to two and a half years in prison.[16] The criminals escaped justice or received minor punishments; the dead youngster's mother, a very well known Solidarity activist, and her attorney were harassed by the authorities, who accused them of aiding people charged with criminal offenses.

The biggest human rights scandal resulted from the police murder of a prominent Solidarity activist, Father Jerzy Popiełuszko, who was beaten to death and his body thrown into a reservoir by functionaries of the internal security forces in an attempt to conceal the crime. The case received so much attention, especially because it involved a priest, that the regime decided to try publicly the low-level police officers directly involved in the murder. The trial, however, had a more political than a judicial character. The defense frequently accused Father Popiełuszko with counterrevolutionary activities and service for foreign intelligence agencies, and the entire Roman Catholic hierarchy in Poland was blamed for promoting antistate activities.

The trial reflected an internal power struggle among the ruling circles in Poland; General Jaruzelski used this incident to place tighter control over the security forces, which had frequently embarrassed his regime by torturing political figures or by attacking or arresting Western tourists. The conflict between the military and the internal security forces, a phenomenon typical of any communist-style regime, was very acute in Poland after the imposition of martial law. The police resented the secondary political role assigned to them by the military and resented the authorities' alleged softness in dealing with the opposition. The Father Popiełuszko affair (which resulted in relatively soft sentences of from two to fifteen years) brought the security forces under much closer supervision by the political leadership, and ended the Mafia-style murders and cross-purpose actions. However, this change came too late to significantly improve

Jaruzelski's image as the man responsible for crimes against the Polish nation.

Father Popiełuszko became a martyr and symbol of opposition to the regime. His grave in Warsaw became a site of pilgrimage for both Poles and foreign visitors, including official representatives of the Western states, who with few exceptions laid flowers on his grave as a symbol of solidarity with Poland's struggle against communist oppression. Among the foreign officials who paid homage to Father Popiełuszko was U.S. vice-president George Bush, who during his trip to Warsaw in October 1987 addressed a group of spontaneously assembled Polish people standing beside the grave.[17] Pope John Paul II, during his 1987 visit to Poland, described Father Popiełuszko as a role model for other Poles to follow.[18]

The peaceful and humanitarian aspirations of the Polish people received prestigious international recognition in 1983, when Lech Wałęsa, the worker who peacefully organized the working class against party domination, received the Nobel Peace Prize. This was a moral victory for Solidarity over the martial law authorities. In Poland, where many developments have to be judged from a long-term historical perspective, such an acknowledgment of national aspirations has an enormous impact that will last for many generations. Political and military setbacks are considered to be temporary and generally insignificant unless there is a lasting effect on the cultural identity of the nation. Wałęsa's Nobel Peace Prize gave the Polish people a sense of triumph. In the minds of many Polish people, the moral victory over communism had already been achieved, and political success was on the way. Marxism-Leninism was losing credibility in the world, and since it also was unable to expand economically, its decline was seen as inevitable. Leszek Kolakowski, an internationally known Polish philosopher now at Oxford University, summarized the rise of Solidarity by stating that "for the first time, a communist government has been forced to wage war on its own society under that name, thus demonstrating in a spectacular fashion the total bankruptcy of communism in the economic, ideological, and social sense. It is a new and perhaps decisive phase in the history of Sovietism, announcing the collapse of the empire as well as of its ideological foundations."[19]

The roots of the Polish crisis lay in Poland's mismanaged national economy. The mismanagement began immediately after World War II, when the country was economically exploited by the Soviet Union. Moscow imposed adoption of the Soviet economic model, excessive spending for defense, and Polish deliveries of coal to the USSR for about 15 percent of the world price. Communist policies resulted in economic stagnation and technological backwardness, which the Sierek-Jaroszewicz team in the

1970s decided to overcome through heavy borrowings from the West. For the first few years the investment boom brought spectacular results in the form of increased exports and a higher standard of living. Soon, however, an imbalance between imports and exports, combined with an uncontrolled growth of consumption and with discriminatory practices against the private sector in agriculture, damaged the national economy to the point that the only remedy left was a sharp price increase on basic consumer goods. This was the immediate cause of the workers' revolt in summer 1980 and the appearance of Solidarity. By the end of 1982, the gross national product had declined by at least 30 percent since 1978, with a production drop of more than 50 percent in certain industries, such as metallurgy, automobiles, and shipbuilding. The economic crisis of 1978–82 completely erased an entire decade of labor by the Polish workers.[20]

The dim legacy of the economic mistakes of the 1970s was not confined to a dramatic decline in production and living standards. By late 1980 Poland owed 460 Western banks a total of $16.2 billion, and $5.35 billion was due for repayment by the end of the year. By comparison, the Polish debt was about $7.5 billion in 1975 and $10.9 at the end of 1979.[21] With hardly any earnings from its exports to the West, Poland had to borrow to pay the interest on its debt; yet the regime continued to purchase food, drugs, raw materials, and spare parts on credit. Rescheduling the huge foreign debt had become one of the major items on Poland's foreign policy agenda. About 60 percent of the Polish debt consisted of loans that were not guaranteed by Western governments. Twenty percent of these loans were received from 60 American banks and the rest from West European, Japanese, and Arab banks. The other 40 percent of the Polish debt consisted of government-guaranteed loans.[22] When Poland failed to make the scheduled payments on these loans between 1982 and 1984, the U.S. Treasury Department had to pay almost $1 billion of the taxpayers' money to American banks.[23]

As long as the Polish government treated the opposition in a manner that was politically acceptable to the Western democracies, the West's enormous sympathy for the Polish people facilitated reschedulings and additional credits. This emotional credit was lost with the introduction of martial law, leaving General Jaruzelski with another problem—coping with the Western bankers.

Poland's economic situation was further complicated by the economic sanctions imposed by the United States and other Western countries. With the foreign debt growing by at least $1 billion annually, Polish trade with the West dropped from about $7.5 billion in 1980 to slightly more than $1 billion in 1983. At the same time, the United States blocked Poland's application for membership in the International Monetary Fund, and Poland's indebtedness to the Soviet-bloc countries was growing rapidly—reaching close to four billion transferable rubles in 1984 and more than five billion a year later.[24] Economic sanctions, and the loss of most-favored-nation status vis-à-vis the United States, hindered the expansion of Polish export industries, and the country's hard-currency earnings and foreign credits practically dried up. Before 1980, Poland could borrow up to $8 billion annually; it received $4.9 billion in 1981, $1.6 billion in 1982, $560 million in 1983, and only about $300 million in 1984–85.[25] The easy life on Western credit was over.

An additional and unexpected economic complication was caused by the nuclear accident at Chernobyl. Warsaw reported substantial hard-currency losses when sixteen Western European countries and the United States, Canada, and Japan restricted the importation of Polish agricultural products in fear of radioactive contamination. Polish officials estimated a decline in foreign sales and tourism of between $35 and $56 million, which prompted Moscow to buy 12,000 tons of Polish beef and pay in hard currency. Poland's earnings from food exports to the West amounted to about $642 million in both 1981 and 1982, $711 million in 1983, $829 million in 1984, and $938 million in 1985. In 1986, the country anticipated a $1.5 billion profit, but following the Chernobyl accident the estimate was reduced to $1 billion.[26] A plausible estimate of Poland's hard-currency losses owing to the Soviet mishap is at least half a billion dollars worth of exports. This price does not include domestic losses of foodstuffs or expenditure on medical supplies, which the regime in Warsaw never made public.

This individual case of economic hardship caused by the Soviets dwarfs the trade inequalities that existed between Poland and the USSR. Polish industrial equipment, built in part with credits provided by Western banks, was imported by the Soviet Union, and paid for in rubles that could not be converted to hard currency. The pricing system within CMEA also favored the USSR, resulting in heavy Polish subsidies of the Soviet economy. In times of crisis, however, Moscow was forced to underwrite the Polish economy. It is estimated that Solidarity's cost to the Soviets exceeded $5 billion in subsidies for Poland just during 1980–81. But because economic relations between the two countries were one of Poland's top state secrets, the actual balance sheet was unknown.

Two more recent changes in Polish-Soviet economic relations contributed to the economic difficulties in Poland. First, starting in 1984 Poland was committed to providing Moscow with credits of about 900 billion zloty ($10 billion) over a fifteen-year period to finance investments in the USSR, in exchange for a share of future production. As Zdzisław Rurarz explained, "This development represents a sharp reversal of the practices of the recent past, when beginning in 1980 the USSR provided Poland with credit. Not only is this era over, but the roles have now been reversed."[27] Poland apparently could no longer count on Soviet credits, as Moscow began to insist on balanced trade relations with Poland.[28]

The second change in Polish-Soviet economic relations involves the price of Soviet commodities exported to Poland. In the past the prices of Soviet oil, natural gas, iron ore, and other basic raw materials were set at an average of the world market prices over the previous three years. In effect, since world prices tended to rise from year to year, Poland and other East European states would pay slightly less than the market price for supplies from the Soviet Union, even with the artificially high value of the ruble against the Western currencies. When the price of oil began to decline in the late 1970s, however, this system of pricing forced Poland to pay higher than world market prices for Soviet energy.

These detrimental economic developments came on top of the fact that the Soviet Union had imposed on Poland a socialist economic system. The indigenous economy, which had been consistent with national tradition and cultural attitudes, was replaced with an unworkable, and socially and environmentally devastating, production of industrial equipment needed almost exclusively in heavy industry and the military. This lopsided energy- and labor-intensive economy was unable to balance the purchasing power of the population with production of desirable consumer goods, including food and other basic commodities. Periodically, the market had to be drained of an excessive supply of money. This was done by means of sudden, painful price increases that frequently provoked strikes. This notorious practice was the only real economic reform practiced by the communists.

Following the introduction of martial law, price increases were frequently combined with big raises for employees in the enterprises that were the most critical to the national economy or the most politically sensitive—all as production declined. The net result of General Jaruzelski's politics and economic practices was that more than 60 percent of the population ended up living below the poverty level. Measured by the black market value of the dollar, the inflation rate was 1,500 percent over a five-year period from 1982 to 1987.

It was well understood in Warsaw that the Soviet Union was unable, or perhaps unwilling, to help improve Poland's standard of living. The Polish authorities themselves had neither a political nor an economic program to deal with the prolonged crisis—only an enormous increase in consumer prices. In fall 1987 the regime invented a new method of seeking popular acceptance for a 110 percent price hike, by calling for a national referendum. Polish voters were asked to support a three-year program of severe economic austerity in exchange for an ambiguously presented plan "of the profound democratization of political life, the aim of which is to strengthen self-government, widen the rights of citizens, and increase citizens' participation in governing the country."[29]

The only positive aspect of the scheme was the public recognition of a link between democratization and economic well-being. The political concessions offered by the authorities failed to go beyond the old slogan of "democratization," which in the communist lexicon means the strengthening of party rule. Hopes for a major breakthrough in the form of an official recognition of socialist pluralism did not materialize. Socialist pluralism would legalize some form of political opposition, perhaps a free and independent trade union, and would impose constraints on the communist monopoly of power. The authorities were still unprepared to admit to the pluralistic nature of Polish society, however, even knowing that no other political move would bring hope and release the creative energy of the nation. The government lost the referendum. It was officially admitted that only 63.8 percent of eligible voters went to the polls; of these only 44 percent supported the price increase and 46 percent favored "democratization." Independent sources put popular participation in the referendum at about 30 percent.[30]

Poland needed authentic democratization and extensive economic assistance from the West to overcome its debilitating crisis. Membership in the IMF, gained in late 1986, offered some hope of acquiring hard currency and the managerial skills that would prevent another waste of billions of dollars on irrational investments, the personal pleasures of the ruling elite, subsidies for unproductive industries, and food subsidies. Technically, the country was eligible for loans totaling over $4 billion, but the unstable political situation and chaotic economy delayed the implementation of Poland's rights as an IMF member. Meanwhile, foreign-debt growth accelerated, approaching the astronomical amount of $40 billion in 1987.

Poland was in political and economic decline, and no positive action was taken to avert a cataclysmic turn that would split the nation apart in a suicidal confrontation. Jaruzelski's regime was so entangled in its own affairs—which included personal power struggles, perfection of police methods, and intrabloc relations (primarily with Moscow)—that its sensitivity to the needs and aspirations of the Polish people appeared to be crippled. It seemed unable to learn from its mistakes, or from those of its predecessors, as it presided over the biggest peacetime crisis ever recorded in an industrialized society.

The Catholic church became the sociopolitical center of Polish national life under communist rule. Poland's religious revival was the result of many causes, including more than 1,000 years of Christian tradition strongly incorporated into Polish culture, and the election of Cardinal Karol Woytyla as Pope John Paul II. The church acquired such enormous moral authority and popularity that on several occasions it was used to calm the nation revolting against its communist rulers. A sui generis symbiosis emerged between the party and the church; although the two institutions competed for influence in Poland, both were united by their determination to save the country from civil strife and Soviet invasion. During domestic crises the church automatically assumed a stabilizing role, helping the authorities to contain the crises within limits acceptable to Moscow and assisting the opposition to win the maximum concessions possible under the circumstances.

The church sided with Solidarity and worked closely with the union, but carefully avoided excessive identification with it. When Solidarity was eliminated as a legal organization, the church once again found itself the only center of opposition. Its policy in the post—martial law era focused on promoting three goals: encouraging real dialogue between the party and the opposition; promoting cultural life independent from the regime; and assisting the private sector of Poland's economy, particularly agriculture.

The church was guided in its approach to Polish politics by the realistic conclusion that Poland's geostrategic location left relatively few political options open, but that the conditions existed for greater popular participation in political affairs. According to the church, the nation was not destined to evolve along the path of Soviet-type socialism; instead it should return through appropriate domestic and foreign policies to its central place in European politics, between East and West. Consequently, Poland's sensitivity to Soviet security interests in Europe should be balanced with a domestic system that represents the democratic aspirations of the Polish people. The most immediate task of the regime, according to the church, was to recognize the pluralistic nature of Polish society and develop sociopolitical structures that would enable the people to participate in decision making. As the first step in this direction, the church insisted that a genuine dialogue be opened between the regime and the nation. The church's position was that the internal state of war would never end without honest, two-way negotiations.

The church's political philosophy went beyond the immediate task of arranging contacts between society and the authorities. The long-range strategy of the church called for a direct challenge to the Marxist-Leninist state in the name of human rights. According to Catholic doctrine human rights, which were bequeathed by God to mankind, are violated by communist regimes that reduce human beings to mere appendages of the workplace. The communist authorities, according to Cardinal Josef

Glemp, the primate of Poland, were engaged in forceful "efforts to erase . . . the values that are most important" for mankind.[31]

The communist authorities were viewed by the church as illegitimate foreign intruders that did not represent the Polish people, but rather were the watchdogs of Soviet strategic and ideological ambitions in Europe. The communist regime was seen as similar to the foreign rule of Poland during the partitions in the nineteenth century. Polish patriotism, therefore, could no longer be linked to the authorities.[32] The scope of church-state cooperation was strictly limited to issues related to national survival under the Soviet hegemony in Eastern Europe, and to joint efforts to combat some of the most devastating social problems, such as poverty and alcoholism.

The essence of the liberation theology professed by the Catholic church in Poland was individual freedom from the totalitarian control of the communist state. During his 1987 visit to Poland, Pope John Paul II lectured the communist authorities on human rights, stressing the relationship between the individual and peace. "If you want to keep peace," stated the pontiff, "remember about man, remember about his rights, that are inalienable, as they result from the very humanity of every human being. Also remember his right to religious freedom of expression."[33]

The church was on the ideological offensive, challenging both the legitimacy of the state and the Marxist-Leninist system of values as incompatible with the Polish national tradition and with human dignity. Consequently, relations between state and church were tense despite cooperation in a few areas. The pattern of coexistence and confrontation continued after the military takeover in 1981, with both sides seeking maximum advantage and minimum compromise, and delaying a showdown to some future time. The two institutions needed each other to protect the country from external and internal dangers; both were competing to influence the future political profile of Poland. General Jaruzelski took it for granted that the next generation of Poles would live in socialism and atheism; the church considered Christianity both the essence of Poland and a guarantee that future generations would live in a democratic and fully independent state. *Tygodnik powszechny*, the most prominent Catholic publication in Poland, described the church as "the heir and trustee of the 1,000 years of national tradition," and presented Christianity as "the spokesman for the working man on both the personal plane and the social plane."[34]

The church was confident that communism not only had exhausted its creative energy, but had generated an economic crisis that could never be reversed as long as the party ruled Poland. Frontal attack on the communist state, could not succeed owing to the enormous military power at the disposal of the communist authorities. Thus, only an evolutionary development away from the socioeconomic patterns of communism could succeed as a long-range strategy of liberation. The church saw the political structures at the top as less important to the national future than cultural preferences, ethical values, and economic issues. Weakened by its oppressive character and its inability to dominate Poland's socioeconomic life, the Polish communist state was seen as being in retreat, leaving a vacuum that would be filled by the church or by some other independent organization.

The regime, facing growing opposition to communism, looked for a clearly defined working relationship with the church, which it saw as a permanent feature on Poland's political horizon. The party hoped to benefit from the political prestige of the church, use its connection with the Western states to secure economic aid for Poland, and be able to permit opposition groups to organize under the auspices of the church. The Roman Catholic hierarchy, however, was reluctant to cooperate with the authorities, for fear of losing its freedom to maneuver and to monitor the opposition. Closer ties with the church would have supported the regime's claim that pluralism existed in Poland, without the necessity of actually sharing power with an organized force that, like Solidarity, could defy the party by calling for free elections. The church avoided any endorsement of communist policies or involvement with the implementation of General Jaruzelski's programs of normalization and political reform. The church cautiously navigated a neutral course of political noninvolvement except in emergency situations when national security was at stake. Any identification of the church with communist policies might have implied that the Roman Catholic hierarchy tacitly accepted the leading role of the party and the irreversibility of communism in Poland.

In post–martial law Poland the social involvement of the church was intensive and successful in providing patronage for independent cultural development. There were more than 14,000 churches and chapels in Poland that provided a place of worship as well as sites for educational services and cultural events such as art exhibitions, film festivals, and concerts. The Catholic press published 31 newspapers with a combined circulation of more than one million copies. These, with the underground publications, were the best guarantees that Poles would be well informed about internal and foreign affairs. Church sponsorship of Polish culture was an effective weapon against Sovietization; it assured ideological pluralism despite the official allegiance to Marxism-Leninism.

The church was less successful in its attempt to sponsor an agricultural foundation that would transfer Western equipment directly to Poland's private farmers. This project, first proposed in 1982, envisioned channeling up to $2 billion in subsidies for Polish farmers and small craftsmen to modernize their productive capacities. The main points of disagreement between the church and the authorities were, first, whether Western assistance should be made available to collective and state-owned enterprises known for their low efficiency; and, second, whether the state should coadminister the foundation with the church. From the beginning the church strongly objected to both propositions. It was unwilling to pay for a government-run agricultural sector of the national economy, and refused to share access to hard currency with the regime, which was burdened with a mishandled foreign debt that had risen to $20 billion in less than a decade.[35]

Negotiations between church and state continued for almost four years until September 1986 when the church became frustrated by the regime's unwillingness to allow any truly independent organization to operate in Poland.[36] After their experience with Solidarity, the authorities were ultrasensitive about any form of large-scale organization functioning outside the party's control.

In conclusion, the regime of General Jaruzelski gave priority to the political objectives of the communist state. For this reason, it took five years for his government to re-create the domestic conditions that would satisfy the West and lead to a resumption of economic relations. During that time the country's dependence on the Soviet Union grew rapidly, and the backlog of unsolved social and economic problems grew unmanageably. A sense of approaching catastrophe became widespread, as did a sense of frustration over society's inability to convince the authorities that without political reforms leading to a pluralistic political system in Poland, the country was heading for a dead end. Polish society was not fooled by the new facade and the minor concessions that did nothing to restrict the monopoly of the communist party. Poland's political impasse pitted the regime, armed with tanks and nightsticks, against the opposition, committed to nonviolent resistance and supported by the great majority of society. General Jaruzelski's regime was a minority government, very insecure at home, and under constant scrutiny—by Moscow, for compliance with Soviet standards; and by the West, which demanded respect for human rights. Facing so many challenges, the Polish authorities were unable to meet either domestic or international expectations; they seemed to react to events rather than charting a clear political course.

The regime sponsored several changes in the political and economic framework of the Polish state. In principle, it recognized the pluralistic character of Polish society and the necessity of granting some degree of influence to noncommunist social forces. Changes in the law on trade unions and territorial self-government, amendments to the electoral law, the decentralization of decision making in the public sector, and the proliferation of private enterprises were indications of a changing perception of reality by the communist authorities and of their inclination to open up the system to the society.

Without compromising with the society, however, the communist party in Poland had no political or economic means available to revive the economy and stimulate public interest in politics. Polish society was deeply divided, distrustful of the authorities, and unwilling to make sacrifices for the sake of future economic gains or ambiguous promises of democratization. Only a decisive breakthrough that would allow a "loyal opposition" to organize and actively participate in governing the country could reverse Poland's socioeconomic decline.

Meanwhile, Solidarity survived the period of martial law, which destroyed its organizational structure but left intact the social movement it represented. Solidarity became a means of self-organization and continued to exist as "an ideal deeply rooted in the population."[37] Public attacks and the arrest of opposition leaders constantly reminded society about the vitality of the union that officially did not exist and was "incapable of working out a real program of action," being limited to "negative destruction, and making their presence known by trying to prevent normal life in the country."[38] The "carrots and sticks" policy continued as the regime tried to intimidate the opposition and overcome social apathy at the same time. The arrest of over 350 opposition leaders in early 1986 was followed by a general amnesty.

Solidarity adopted three distinct strategies for dealing with the authorities. First, it followed a policy of "everything or nothing," that is, of either strong pressure or total inaction. Second, the union was committed to searching for a meaningful dialogue with the regime. Third, the union was determined to win not "through armed combat but through development," in the words of Lech Wałęsa.[39]

The regime decided to show initiative by offering referendum on the reforms. Its purpose was to motivate the people, to outmaneuver Solidarity, and to provide the general public with a chance to vote. Polish voters were asked to approve or disapprove two vaguely formulated programs: the first concerned the radical healing of the economy and the improvement of living standards in three years; the second advocated democratization and self-government.[40] These deceptively phrased objectives were intended to justify huge price increases and restore the legitimacy of the communist party. The party was ready to sacrifice some of its decision-making powers in exchange for recognition of its supremacy.

This expensive and elaborate facade of democracy failed to fool the public, however. As has already been noted, only 63.8 percent of all eligible to vote participated in the referendum, and of those who voted 44 percent supported the economic proposition and 46 percent were in favor of the political program offered by the party.[41] The regime admitted defeat and finally realized that acting alone it would never be able to reform the nation's economy or mobilize society to work.

In spring and summer 1988, Poland was again paralyzed by a wave of strikes at the shipyards, coal mines, and steel mills. The old idea of dialogue with the union was revived as a means of broadening the social base of the regime. Changes of ministers and prime ministers in Poland having had no effect on the political consensus, the government proceeded to reestablish contacts with Solidarity. At the initial meetings between Lech Wałęsa, chairman of the outlawed Solidarity, and Czeslaw Kiszczak, a member of the ruling Politburo and minister of internal affairs, it was agreed that full-scale "roundtable" negotiations would begin in mid-October 1988.[42]

Opposition within the party to the new contract with Solidarity succeeded in frustrating the first deadline. Mieczysław Rakowski, Poland's new prime minister, insisted that his government would negotiate only with a "constructive" opposition and that "the search for a broad agreement does not lead to Wałęsa . . . and a few others who consider themselves leaders of the opposition. We are looking for the active participation of a lot of people who have a totally different view than the current leadership of Solidarity."[43]

Negotiations with the union broke down when the authorities objected to the inclusion of two prominent activists, Jacek Kuron and Adam Michnik, among the delegates.[44] An additional provocation was the decision to close the Lenin shipyard, the cradle of Solidarity.[45] The move was calculated to uproot the union as well as to divert its attention from national issues of a political nature to basic bread-and-butter concerns.

It was soon discovered that by undermining the basic security of the workers the government was inviting a new wave of strikes that would certainly spread throughout the country. In exchange for the union's pledge to refrain from strikes as a political weapon, the regime dropped all preconditions for negotiations with the union, returning after seven painful years to the situation that had existed before martial law.

Postscript

Years of repeated failure to improve the Polish economy and stabilize the explosive social situation finally convinced the regime of the necessity of real dialogue with the opposition. The two-month-long "round table" negotiations produced a new social contract in Poland. On 5 April 1989, Solidarity and the government signed accords restoring the union's legal status and providing for the first free elections since World War II. After more than 40 years, the country was allowed to exercise its right to the "free and unfettered" elections guaranteed by the Yalta accord.

The 4 June elections resulted in a landslide victory for Solidarity. Under the pre-electoral agreement between Solidarity and the communist authorities, the regime secured for itself a 65 percent majority in the Sejm, the lower house of the legislative body in Poland; but all 100 seats in the newly created Senate were contested freely. In the two stages of the electoral process, the communist party and its allies lost all of the 161 contested seats in the Sejm and 99 out of the 100 seats in the Senate. Without the guarantee of 65 percent in the Sejm, the party would have been completely swept from power.

Poland's evolution from communism has entered a new stage with the transition from a one-party state to a multiparty parliamentary government. Impoverished Poland has begun to emerge from the darkness of the communist system. The country is expected to strive for a West European type of political system anchored in free elections, a free press, and an independent judiciary. Economically, Poland is moving toward free enterprise and has hopes of eventual membership in the European Community. In the international arena, Poland is expected to opt for neutrality protected by both superpowers.

This unprecedented departure from the fundamental principles of Soviet totalitarianism could not have happened without approval from Moscow. The Polish authorities have the full support of the Soviet leadership headed by Secretary Gorbachev. The Soviet Union has established contacts with Solidarity, adopting in practice a dual approach to Poland. This development is an explicit departure from the Brezhnev Doctrine, which was invoked to justify the invasion of Czechoslovakia in 1968 and the "lesser evil" of martial law in Poland in 1981. The current Soviet leadership has not attempted to enforce conformity in Eastern Europe. The Soviets are concerned only with Poland's respect for international agreements.

The transition from a one-party communist state to a semidemocratic political system could not have occurred without an active involvement by the United States on behalf of democratic forces in Poland. The United States provided hope and legitimacy for the antitotalitarian forces in Poland, and kept alive the expectation that democratization would open the door to substantial economic assistance from the West. At the same time, the U.S. policy toward Poland was designed to accommodate the legitimate security interests of the USSR in Eastern Europe. This approach produced a considerable degree of harmony and cooperation between the two superpowers. The benign attitude of the West toward the democratic changes in Poland made it easier for Moscow to accept the de-Sovietization of Eastern Europe, since these developments were not seen as either humiliating to the Soviets or a danger to their security in Europe.

Political changes in Poland can now be expected to assume secondary importance, since the main focus of attention has shifted to economic and social matters. For this reason, the final success of democracy in Poland is far from certain. Failure to reverse the economic crisis would have a catastrophic impact on the Polish nation, which would be in danger of falling victim to totalitarian extremists once more. Such a failure would undoubtedly be fatal to Gorbachev's experiments with *glasnost'* and *perestroika,* giving legitimacy to the neo-Stalinist forces in the USSR.

Peaceful Finlandization of Poland is in the best interest of the two superpowers and the West European states.

Notes

All quotations taken directly from foreign-language sources have been translated by the author.

Chapter One. Moscow and the Independent Trade Union in Poland

1. *Pravda,* 20 August 1980; Quoted in Radio Free Europe–Radio Liberty, hereafter, RFE-RL, *Radio Liberty Research,* 302/80, 27 August 1980.
2. *Trybuna ludu,* 30–31 August 1980.
3. *Washington Post,* 7 September 1980.
4. Quoted in RFE-RL, *Radio Liberty Research* 24/80, 5 November 1980.
5. *Washington Post,* 31 October 1980.
6. Radio Free Europe Research, *RAD Background Report* 222, 17 September 1980.
7. *Trybuna ludu,* 1 November 1980.
8. Quoted in RFE-RL, *Radio Liberty Research* 436/80, 16 November 1980.
9. Quoted in RFE-RL, *Radio Liberty Research* 435/80, 13 November 1980.
10. Quoted in RFE-RL, *Radio Liberty Research* 480/80, 12 December 1980.

11. *Christian Science Monitor,* 8 December 1980.
12. Alex Alexiev, A. Ross Johnson, and S. Enders Wimbush, *The Soviets Invade Poland* (Santa Monica, Calif.: Rand Corporation, 1980), pp. 3–4; and *U.S. News and World Report,* 15 December 1980.
13. Professor John Erickson of Edinburgh University, quoted in *Newsweek,* 15 December 1980.
14. *Christian Science Monitor,* 8 December 1980.
15. *Handelsbad,* Rotterdam, 8 December 1980.
16. *New York Times,* 24 December 1980.
17. *Christian Science Monitor,* 3 December 1980.
18. *Washington Star,* 2 January 1981.
19. *Trybuna ludu,* 29 December 1980.
20. *Krasnaya zvezda,* 14 March 1981.
21. *Krasnaya zvezda,* 25 March 1981.
22. *Pravda,* 2 April 1981; *Izvestiia,* 5 April 1981.
23. Quoted in RFE-RL, *Radio Liberty Research* 225/81, 2 June 1981.
24. The full text of the CPSU Central Committee letter to the Polish Central Committee on 5 June 1981 was published by *Le Monde,* 10 June 1981.
25. *Christian Science Monitor,* 12 June 1981.
26. *Trybuna ludu,* 4 July 1981.
27. *Pravda,* 16 July 1981.
28. *New York Times,* 21 July 1981.
29. *Washington Post,* 23 September 1981.
30. *Pravda,* 10 January 1982.
31. *New York Times,* 14 December 1981.
32. *Literaturnaya gazeta,* 1 January and 10 February 1981.
33. *Washington Post,* 31 December 1981.
34. *Pravda,* 5 January 1982.
35. Tass, 12 January 1982; *Trybuna ludu,* 13 January 1982.

Chapter Two. Restoration of the Status Quo

1. *Novo vremyé,* 2 March 1982.
2. *Washington Post,* 29 August 1982.
3. Warsaw Domestic Television Service, 20 August 1982; quoted in Foreign Broadcast Information Service–East Europe, hereafter, *FBIS-EEU,* 23 August 1982.
4. *Trybuna ludu,* 9 September 1983.
5. *Question of the Violations of Human Rights and Fundamental Freedoms in Any Part of the World, with Particular Reference to Colonial and Other De-*

pendent Territories. Report on the Situation in Poland, presented by Undersecretary-general Hugo Gobbi (United Nations, 1983).

6. Warsaw Domestic Television Service, 1 March 1983; quoted in *FBIS-EEU,* 2 March 1983.
7. *Trybuna ludu,* 14 May 1983.
8. *Le Figaro,* 12 May 1983.
9. *Trybuna ludu,* 12 July 1984.
10. Ibid., 11 June 1984.
11. Ibid., 10 April 1984.
12. Ibid., 23 June 1984.
13. *Washington Post,* 29 November 1984.
14. *Trybuna ludu,* 27 September 1984.
15. *Rzeczpospolita,* 12 November 1984.
16. *Le Figaro,* 9 May 1984.
17. *Trybuna ludu,* 7 May 1984.
18. *Trybuna ludu,* 9 January 1986.
19. Havana Domestic Service, 17 September 1985, quoted in *FBIS-EEU,* 18 September 1985.
20. Mikhail S. Gorbachev, quoted in the *Washington Post,* 28 April 1985.
21. Anna Swidlicka, in Radio Free Europe Research, Polish SR/8, 21 May 1985.
22. *Le Figaro,* 15 July 1986; *The Baltimore Sun,* 3 July 1986.
23. "Poland Today, The State of the Republic." Report of the Experience and Future (Discussion Group), London: Pluto Press, 1981, p. 112.
24. *The New York Times,* 9 March 1986.
25. *Trybuna ludu,* 1–2 March 1986.
26. *Washington Post,* 12 November 1987.
27. *Rzeczpospolita,* 13 July 1988.
28. *Trybuna ludu,* 28 April 1989.
29. *Polityka,* 22 July 1989.
30. *Washington Post,* 26 November 1989.

Chapter Three. United States Support for Solidarity

1. *New York Times,* 14 September 1980.
2. *New York Times,* 28 August 1980.
3. Quoted in the *New York Times,* 10 September 1980.
4. *Christian Science Monitor,* 8 December 1980.
5. *New York Times,* 11 September 1980.

6. Quoted in the *New York Times*, 10 September 1980.

7. *Trybuna ludu*, 10 December 1980.

8. U.S. Department of State, Bureau of Public Affairs, Current Policy no. 271 (29 March 1981).

9. *New York Times*, 27 March 1981.

10. *New York Times*, 3 April 1981.

11. *New York Times*, 19 July 1981.

12. *New York Times*, 11 June 1981.

13. *New York Times*, 12 June 1981.

14. *New York Times* 19 July 1981.

15. *New York Times*, 5 June 1981.

16. *Pravda*, 25 December 1981.

17. See note 9, above.

18. Quoted in *FBIS-EEU*, 30 December 1981.

19. *Żołnierz wolności*, 29 January 1982.

20. *Trybuna ludu*, 10 December 1981.

21. *Christian Science Monitor*, 29 December 1981.

22. *Washington Post*, 29 December 1981.

23. *Pravda*, 27 December 1981.

24. *Pravda*, 25 December 1981.

25. *Pravda*, 27 December 1981.

26. *Trybuna ludu*, 25 December 1981.

Chapter Four. Economic Sanctions

1. *Department of State Bulletin* 82, no. 2059 (1982).

2. *New York Times*, 12 January 1982.

3. *Trybuna ludu*, 3 November 1983.

4. *Rzeczpospolita*, 8 November 1983.

5. *Congressional Record*, 9 February 1982.

6. *Żołnierz wolności*, 29 January 1982.

7. Ibid., 3 May 1982.

8. *Novo vremyé*, 27 January 1982.

9. *World Affairs* 144, no. 4 (1982).

10. *Department of State Bulletin* 82, no. 2068 (1982).

11. *The Times* (London), 16 February 1982.

12. *Christian Science Monitor*, 23 August 1982.

13. *Trybuna ludu,* 27 September 1982.
14. *New York Times,* 11 May 1982.
15. *Weekly Compilation of Presidential Documents* 18, no. 41 (9 October 1982).
16. *Trybuna ludu,* 29 October 1982.
17. *Historic Documents of 1982* (Washington, D.C.: Congressional Quarterly, Inc., 1983), pp. 950–52.
18. *Trybuna ludu,* 4–5 December 1982.
19. *Polityka Stanow Ziednoczonych Ameryki Wobec Polski W Swietle Faktow i Dokumentow (1980–1983)* (Warsaw: Polski Instytut Spraw Miedzynarodowych, Instytut Badania Wspolczesnych Problemow Kapitalizmu, 1984), pp. 122–25.
20. *Trybuna ludu,* 12 March 1983.
21. *Życie warszawy,* 2 March 1983.
22. *Rzeczpospolita,* 1 June 1983.
23. *Trybuna ludu,* 27 August 1983.
24. *Rzeczpospolita,* 5 December 1983.
25. *Trybuna ludu,* 18 August 1983.
26. *Trybuna ludu,* 4 November 1983.
27. Ibid.
28. *Życie warszawy,* 7 December 1983.
29. *New York Times,* 20 January 1984.
30. *Rzeczpospolita,* 12 December 1983.
31. *Trybuna ludu,* 30 July 1984.
32. *New York Times,* 6 August 1984.
33. *Wall Street Journal,* 24 July 1984.
34. *Weekly Compilation of Presidential Documents* 20, no. 32 (17 August 1984).
35. Ibid., no. 37 (9 September 1984).
36. *Rzeczpospolita,* 3 September 1984.
37. *Trybuna ludu,* 20 October 1984.
38. "U.S. Relations with Poland," U.S. Department of State, Bureau of Public Affairs, Current Policy no. 621 (11 October 1984).
39. Quoted in *Rzeczpospolita,* 13 February 1985.
40. *Rzeczpospolita,* 17 April 1985.
41. *Los Angeles Times,* 3 May 1985.
42. *Trybuna ludu,* 7 May 1985.
43. *Washington Post,* 26 September 1985.
44. *New York Times,* 1 September 1985.
45. *New York Times,* 4 September 1985.
46. *New York Times,* 26 September 1985.

47. *Los Angeles Times,* 27 March 1986.
48. *Żołnierz wolności,* 29 January 1986.
49. *FBIS-EEU,* 16 April 1986.
50. *U.S. News and World Report,* 21 July 1986.
51. Quoted in Radio Free Europe Research, 18 November 1986, pp. 15–16.
52. *Washington Post,* 10 December 1986.
53. *New York Times,* 20 January 1987.
54. *New York Times,* 20 January 1987.
55. *Trybuna ludu,* 10 March 1987.
56. *Życie warszawy,* 11 March 1987.
57. *FBIS-EEU,* 29 July 1987.
58. *Washington Post,* 4 October 1987.
59. Warsaw, Polska Agencja Prasowa (Polish Press Agency), 14 October 1987; quoted in *FBIS-EEU,* 17 October 1987.
60. *Trybuna ludu,* 9 October 1988.
61. *Trybuna ludu,* 13 July 1989.

Chapter Five. From Negotiations to a Military Solution

1. *Trybuna ludu,* 11 December 1980.
2. Radio Free Europe Research, 10 October 1980.
3. *Glos pracy,* 2 September 1980.
4. *New York Times,* 25 October 1980.
5. From an interview in *Der Spiegel,* 4 August 1980.
6. *New York Times,* 17 June 1981.
7. Michael Dobbs, "Political Earthquake," *Washington Post,* 23 July 1981.
8. *The Times* (London), 1 May 1981.
9. *Trybuna ludu,* 25 November 1981.
10. *Trybuna ludu,* 25 December 1981.
11. *La Stampa,* 21 February 1982.
12. *Stern,* 29 January 1982.
13. *L'Humanité,* 25 January 1982.

Chapter Six. The Politics of Self-Destruction

1. *Los Angeles Times,* 14 July 1982.
2. *New York Times,* 19 December 1983.

3. *Le Figaro*, 26 February 1982.

4. *Polityka*, 2 July 1983.

5. *Trybuna ludu*, 19 September 1983.

6. *Trybuna ludu*, 23–24 July 1983.

7. *Le Monde*, 21 December 1982.

8. Ibid.

9. Ibid.

10. *Rzeczpospolita*, 8 August 1983.

11. *Washington Post*, 27 September 1985.

12. *Trybuna ludu*, 23–24 July 1983.

13. *Washington Post*, 7 January 1983.

14. *Trybuna ludu*, 25 August 1983.

15. *Committee in Support of Solidarity Report*, 13 July 1984.

16. *Prawo i życie*, 21 July 1984.

17. *Washington Post*, 4 October 1987.

18. *New York Times*, 1 September 1987.

19. *Le Matin*, 13 December 1982; reprinted in *Joint Publications Research Service*, 16 February 1983.

20. *Kultura* (Paris), no. 11/434, May 1983.

21. *Christian Science Monitor*, 24 July 1981.

22. *New York Times*, 26 June 1981.

23. *New York Times*, 6 August 1984.

24. *Rzeczpospolita*, 23 April 1985.

25. *Rynki zagraniczne*, 12–15 April 1986.

26. *Trybuna ludu*, 13 May 1986.

27. *Wall Street Journal*, 19 June 1985.

28. Radio Free Europe Research, Polish SR/9, 5 June 1985.

29. *Trybuna ludu*, 24–25 October 1987.

30. *FBIS-EEU*, 30 November 1987.

31. *Washington Post*, 27 August 1985.

32. *Tygodnik powszechny*, 10 March 1985.

33. Warsaw Domestic Service, 8 June 1987; quoted in *FBIS-EEU*, 9 June 1987.

34. *Tygodnik powszechny*, 14 June 1986.

35. *Los Angeles Times*, 16 September 1984.

36. *Przeglad Katolicki*, 5 October 1986.

37. Jozef Cardinal Glemp, quoted in *Le Monde*, 13–14 April 1986.

38. *Trybuna ludu*, 15 October 1986.

39. *Neue Kronen Zeitung*, 3 October 1987.

40. *Trybuna ludu*, 24–25 October 1987.

41. *Washington Post,* 30 November 1987.
42. *Washington Post,* 17 September 1988.
43. *Washington Post,* 28 September 1988.
44. *New York Times,* 26 October 1988.
45. *New York Times,* 1 November 1988.

Bibliography

Books

Alexiev, Alex, A. Ross Johnson, and S. Enders Wimbush. *The Soviets Invade Poland*. Santa Monica, Calif.: Rand Corporation, 1980.

American University. *Poland, a Country Study*. Washington, D.C.: American University, Foreign Area Studies, 1983.

Bialer, Seweryn. *The Soviet Paradox*. New York: Vintage Books, 1986.

Brandys, Kazimierz. *A Warsaw Diary: 1978–1981*. New York: Random House, 1983.

Brumberg, Abraham, ed. *Poland: Genesis of a Revolution*. New York: Random House, 1983.

Dawisha, Karen. *Eastern Europe, Gorbachev and Reform*. Cambridge: Cambridge University Press, 1988.

Dawisha, Karen, Lincoln Gordon, and John W. Kiser III. *Change in Eastern Europe: Soviet Interests and Western Opportunities*. Washington, D.C.: Atlantic Council of the United States, 1989.

Flakierski, Henryk. *Economic Reform and Income Distribution: A Case Study of Hungary and Poland*. Armonk, N.Y.: M. E. Sharpe, 1986.

Garton Ash, Timothy. *The Polish Revolution: Solidarity*. New York: Scribner, 1984.

Gordon, Lincoln. *Eroding Empire: Western Relations with Eastern Europe*. Washington, D.C.: Brookings Institution, 1987.

Hough, Jerry F. *The Polish Crisis—American Policy Options: A Staff Paper.* Washington, D.C.: Brookings Institution, 1982.

Jones, Christopher D. *Soviet Influence in Eastern Europe.* New York: Praeger, 1981.

Lineberry, William P., ed. *Poland.* New York: H. W. Wilson, 1984.

Lukas, Richard C. *Bitter Legacy: Polish-American Relations in the Wake of World War II.* Lexington, Ky.: University Press of Kentucky, 1982.

Marer, Paul, and Wlodzimierz Siwinski, eds. *Creditworthiness and Reform in Poland.* Bloomington and Indianapolis: Indiana University Press, 1988.

Ploss, Sidney I. *Moscow and the Polish Crisis: An Interpretation of Soviet Policies and Intentions.* Westview Special Studies on the Soviet Union and Eastern Europe. Boulder, Colo.: Westview Press, 1986.

"Poland Today, The State of the Republic," Report of the Experience and Future (Discussion Group), London: Pluto Press, 1981.

Polityka Stanów Ziednoczonych Ameryki wobec Polski w swietle faktow i dokumentów (1980–1983). Warsaw: Polski Instytut Spraw Miedzynarodwych, Instytut Badania Wspolczesnych Problemow Kapitualizmu, 1984.

United Nations. *Question of the Violations of Human Rights and Fundamental Freedoms in Any Part of the World, with Particular Reference to Colonial and Other Dependent Territories: Report on the Situation in Poland.* Presented by Under secretary-general Hugo Gobbi. 1983.

Sanford, George. *Polish Communism in Crisis: The Politics of Reform and Reaction, 1980–1981.* New York: St. Martin's Press, 1983.

Staar, Richard F. *USSR Foreign Policies after Detente.* Stanford: Hoover Institution Press, 1987.

Staar, Richard F., ed. *Yearbook on International Communist Affairs.* Stanford: Hoover Institution Press, 1981, 1982, 1983, 1984, 1985, 1986, 1987, 1988, 1989.

Szajkowski, Bogdan. *Next to God—Poland: Politics and Religion in Contemporary Poland.* New York: St. Martin's Press, 1983.

Terry, Sarah Meiklejohn, ed. *Soviet Policy in Eastern Europe.* New Haven and London: Yale University Press, 1984.

Touraine, Alain, with Grazyna Gesicka and David Denby. *Solidarity: The Analysis of a Social Movement: Poland, 1980–1981.* Cambridge: Cambridge University Press, 1983.

United States. House. Committee on Foreign Affairs. Subcommittee on Europe and the Middle East. *Poland's Renewal and U.S. Options: A Policy Reconnaissance.* 100th Cong., 1st sess., 1987.

United States. Senate. Committee on Foreign Relations. *Poland: Its Renewal and a U.S. Strategy.* 97th Cong., 1st sees., 1981.

United States. Senate. Committee on Foreign Relations. Subcommittee on European Affairs. *Poland's Roundtable and U.S. Options.* 101st Cong., 1st sess., 1989.

Vine, Richard D., ed. *Soviet–East European Relations as a Problem for the West.* London, New York, Sydney: Croom Helm, 1987.

Weschler, Lawrence. *The Passion of Poland, from Solidarity through the State of War.* New York: Pantheon Books, 1984.

Periodicals

Anderson, Richard D., Jr. "Soviet Decision-Making and Poland." *The Problems of Communism.* March/April 1982.

Avory, William. "Political Legitimacy and Crisis in Poland." *Political Science Quarterly.* Spring 1988.

Barbieri, Frane. "Polonia: Esiste una soluzione?" *Affari esteri.* Winter 1983.

Bialer, Seweryn. "Poland and the Soviet Imperium." *Foreign Affairs.* No. 3 (1981).

Bolshakov, V. "On the U.S. Special Services' Interference in PPR Affairs." *Current Digest of the Soviet Press.* 27 January 1982.

Chesnoff, Richard Z., and Douglas Stanglin. "From a U.S. Mole: Inside Story of What Might Have Been." *U.S. News and World Report.* 20 April 1987.

Cooper, Wendy. "Western Governments Are Calling the Soviets' Bluff over Poland's $27 Billion Debt." *Multinational Monitor.* Fall 1982.

Fromm, Joseph. "Another Lost Cause for the U.S.?" *U.S. News and World Report.* 11 January 1982.

Goldman, Minton F. "Soviet Policy Toward the Political Unrest: Turmoil in Poland during the Fall of 1980." *East European Quarterly.* Fall 1986.

"Gorbachev in Poland, Talks with Jaruzelski." *Current Digest of the Soviet Press.* 10 August 1988.

Gray, John. "Can Warsaw and Moscow Be Friends? Poland Is Still in the Warsaw Pact." *World Press Review.* October 1989.

House, Karen Elliot. "Allies' Choices: What West Will Do If Poland Is Invaded Is Chiefly up to Europe." *Wall Street Journal.* 11 December 1980.

House, Karen Elliot, et al. "Moscow's Dilemma: Polish Events Pressure Russia to Invade, but It Would Face High Cost." *Wall Street Journal.* 4 December 1980.

"Interview with Polish Journalists, June 30, 1989." *Weekly Compilation of Presidential Documents.* 10 July 1989.

Kopvillem, Peeter. "Discouragement and Hope." *Maclean's.* 25 July 1988.

Kraus, Michael. "Soviet Policy toward East Europe." *Current History.* November 1987.

Lange, Peer H. "Polen als Problem sowjetischer Sicherheitspolitik." *Aussenpolitik: Zeitschrift fur internationale Fragen.* No. 4 (1981).

Madison, Christopher. "Should Sanctions End?" *National Journal.* 29 November 1986.

Milewski, Jerzy, Krzysztof Pomian, and Jan Zielonka. "Poland: Four Years After." *Foreign Affairs.* Spring, 1985.

Morawski, Dominik. "L'esperimento polacco." *Affari Esteri.* Spring 1981.

Rachwald, Arthur R. "Poland: Quo Vadis?" *Current History.* November 1982.

Reagan, Ronald. "Solidarity and U.S. Relations with Poland: Radio Address to the Nation, October 9, 1982." *Weekly Compilation of Presidential Documents.* 18 October 1982.

"Resort to Force 'Won't Solve Any Problem' for Kremlin: Interview with Walter Laqueur, Expert on Communist Affairs." *U.S. News and World Report.* 28 December 1981 and 4 January 1982.

Sergeyev, A. "The Hypocritical Intrigues around Poland." *International Affairs.* April 1982.

Staar, Richard F. "Soviet Relations with East Europe." *Current History.* November 1984.

"U.S. Allies Close Ranks on Poland." *U.S. News and World Report.* 22 February 1982.

"U.S. Measures Taken against the Soviet Union Concerning Poland." *Department of State Bulletin.* February 1982.

Valkenier, Elizabeth. "To Tell the Truth." *The New Republic.* 22 May 1989.

Wasowski, Stanislaw S. "U.S. Sanctions against Poland." *The Washington Quarterly.* Spring 1986.

Weiss, Seymour. "The Reagan Response on Poland." *Wall Street Journal.* 29 December 1981.

"Why the Poles Won't Knuckle Under: Interview with Jan Gross, Authority on Polish History and Society." *U.S. News and World Report.* 23 February 1981.

Index

About the Author

Arthur R. Rachwald is an Associate Professor of Political Science at the United States Naval Academy. He received his Ph.D. from the University of California at Santa Barbara and is the recipient of a Naval Academy Research Council grant for research on the Gorbachev doctrine (1989).